Wikis

Wikis

The Educator's Power Tool

Kay Teehan

LINWORTH

AN IMPRINT OF ABC-CLIO, LLC
Santa Barbara, California • Denver, Colorado • Oxford, England

Library of Congress Cataloging-in-Publication Data

Teehan, Kay.
  Wikis : the educator's power tool / Kay Teehan.
    p. cm.
  Includes bibliographical references and index.
  ISBN 978-1-58683-530-9 (acid-free paper) — ISBN 978-1-58683-531-6 (ebook)
  1. Computer-assisted instruction. 2. Internet in education. 3. Electronic encyclopedias. 4. User-generated content. 5. Wikipedia. I. Title.
  LB1028.5.T464 2010
  371.33'44678—dc22   2010020285

ISBN: 978-1-58683-530-9
EISBN: 978-1-58683-531-6

14 13 12 11 10   1 2 3 4 5

This book is also available on the World Wide Web as an eBook.
Visit www.abc-clio.com for details.

Linworth
An Imprint of ABC-CLIO, LLC

ABC-CLIO, LLC
130 Cremona Drive, P.O. Box 1911
Santa Barbara, California 93116-1911

This book is printed on acid-free paper ∞

Manufactured in the United States of America

To my children, Sarah, Tim, Larry, and Greg,
who are the lights of my life.

Contents

Figures

Introduction

Times are tough in schools these days. Lack of funding combined with high-stakes testing standards, curriculum maps, and top-down edicts of teaching strategies have made teaching a very difficult job. Add to all of this the pressure to integrate more technology into the curriculum and the massive amount of Web 2.0 technology tools along with the huge amount of information available for use, and teachers can become overwhelmed. The purpose of this book is to make one of the most powerful tools—the wiki—less mysterious and easy to add to the strategies teachers can utilize to meet new demands on their time and talent.

The book describes three types of wikis, each having a different purpose and outcome. Teachers will find uses for each type, and the advantages of wikis as a learning strategy will become evident to them. Based on 21st-century technology standards, the use of integrated technology tools in student learning is a life skill to assure success in a world where teachers prepare students for jobs that do not yet exist. By following the guidelines in this book, teachers will help students organize, synthesize, and evaluate information they can use for problem solving and higher-level thinking, which are elements that form the basis for achievement in tomorrow's fast-paced, high-stress world.

By using the guidelines found in this book, teachers and media specialists, administrators, and support staff will learn the advantages of using wikis in and out of the classroom. Many real-world examples are included that show how wikis are being used by educational professionals all over the world. To engage and motivate students, I have thoughtfully chosen model wikis that can be used as templates for wiki creations. Please bear in mind that URLs often change or are deleted entirely. I have put all the active links mentioned in these pages on a wiki that I will attempt to keep updated to assure that readers will have access to all the sites referred to.

I have created a support wiki to accompany the content of this book. At this wiki site are live links to the many wiki examples, as well as videos to help you create wikis. Please use this site to complement the guidelines found in this text. You will find this wiki at: <http://educatorspowertool.pbworks.com>. There you will find a wiki page where you can leave comments and messages for me and post the URL of your new wiki to share with others. I would love to communicate with you in your endeavor of implementing wikis in your classroom.

CHAPTER 1

What Is a Wiki?

The 21st-century educator and media specialist have an array of Web 2.0 tools to utilize in their endeavor to make resources available for the students and staff they serve. Web 2.0 is the new generation of the Internet that takes it far beyond isolated Web pages. Web 2.0 is based on user participation that encourages open communication, allows for data to be controlled by many people, and inspires teamwork. In education, it can be used as a vehicle that allows teachers to connect, communicate, and collaborate. Our students use Web 2.0 tools on a daily basis in the form of blogs, tweets, and Facebook postings. Teachers who want to maximize their ability to relate to today's student must know what their students know about technology, and must be able to learn with the same tools students learn with every day.

Although there is a place for all of these tools in the pursuit of their goals, perhaps one of education's greatest tools is the wiki. It is a tool that allows the media specialist and teacher to demonstrate collaborative and leadership skills that serve students in supportive ways. Wikis can be the most effective tool we have in today's educational setting, where time to collaborate face-to-face has almost disappeared.

The word *wiki* derives from a Hawaiian word that means quick. This definition is applicable to this tool, as a wiki is a Web site that can be created in a hurry. Wikis have many uses, among which are managing information, knowledge, and ideas. In today's world of fast-paced, high-pressure, high-stakes learning, educators have a specific need to manage the tremendous amount of information available to their students. We can no longer ignore the fact that the remarkable amount of information, tools, and strategies available to today's teachers and students needs managing and organizing in order to be useful. Wikis can bring order to this information overload phenomena and help students make sense of facts, statistics, details, and data they collect while doing research or even while browsing for information. Moreover, teachers as well as students increasingly need to do this managing in a minimal amount of time, which is precious. They also need a vehicle that is of nominal cost or free to use. (*Free* is the universal keyword to educators everywhere!)

The most well-known and most used wiki today is Wikipedia, which has developed into a huge free, collaborative, Web-based, multilingual encyclopedia. It grows larger every day as users add to the base of knowledge and correct misinformation others have posted there. While the editors strive for accuracy in this source, many articles are not verifiable or are out-and-out wrong. Because the information on Wikipedia cannot be considered authoritative, this wiki has developed a tarnished reputation. While the content is generally factual, many school districts will not allow students to cite Wikipedia articles in research. However, students still tend to gravitate to Wikipedia frequently for their own purposes in gathering information.

Wikipedia is managed by a not-for-profit parent organization, The Wikimedia Foundation. Anyone can contribute individual entries to the wiki, and anyone can edit any entry for biased, out-of-date, or incorrect information. Because there are so many people reading the articles and monitoring contributions, incorrect information is usually corrected quickly. Thus, the overall accuracy of the encyclopedia is improving all the time. According to recent data, Wikipedia has a monthly traffic rate of 2 billion page views. It reports that 50 percent of the users are from countries other than the United States. This is incredible, because Wikipedia does not market its resource in any way. Although it has resisted the temptation (so far) of selling ads and banners on the Wikipedia site, its traffic patterns indicate that it could be one of the biggest Web-based moneymakers in the world if it ever decides to accept advertising. This is all evidence that collaborative wikis have an important place in the 21st century and that people like the idea of being involved in a constantly changing process of creation and collaboration. Nevertheless, Wikipedia has still not gained respectability in academic settings, and its use is banned for most student research projects.

So, given the evidence of popularity of wiki use, what is the value of wikis in education today? Even though today's students are probably the best multitaskers the world has ever produced, the sheer amount of information they take in can be overwhelming and block them from spontaneously doing the higher-level thinking that is required for analysis and synthesis. Educators looking for a method of improving the environment for these students to facilitate information management will find that wikis can provide them with an instrument that will systematize, organize, classify, and categorize knowledge, information, statistics, and ideas. These elements serve to enhance student learning. Wikis are not only beneficial to teachers and media specialists but are extremely helpful to students.

21st-Century Learning Standards

Students are technology-savvy in many areas, but, unfortunately, research is not one of them. Students can easily find the lyrics of the newest rap recording, but they sometimes do not apply those searching skills to doing research for a school assignment. Moreover, if they do stumble onto the subject they want, they often do not have the skills to recognize accurate, unbiased, and current information. In addition, students need to know and be able to utilize certain technology skills to be successful. These skills include:

- **Communication and Collaboration**

One of the most important technology skills that students must learn is how to access information in a digital environment and interact, collaborate, and publish their findings. Communication of what they have learned, how they found the information, and analysis of its meaning will help other students build on the knowledge. Another of the most important skills of the 21st century is learning to work successfully as a team player to solve problems and create new ideas. Because of its effectiveness and productivity, business adopted this work model years ago. Students need to practice collaboration skills they need to be team players and good communicators while engaged in project assignments. This type of assignment gives students practice in the tools that will be important for success in future employment. The use of wikis is a convenient tool to facilitate this goal because of the intrinsic use of communication and collaboration, which are the basis of wiki resources. Wikis enhance the communication process by becoming the vehicle for sharing information, building on other students' knowledge base, and collaborating on new ideas.

- **Research and Information Literacy**

Students need to gather, evaluate, and use information using digital tools. This is an important acquired skill. Strategies to locate, organize, evaluate, analyze, and synthesize the information they need form the basis of students' research skills. Educators need to instruct students in both the value of mastering these research tools and the methods of implementing the strategies themselves. It also is important that students are engaged in the use multimedia artifacts that are relevant to the task they are learning and that they use the data they find in an ethical manner. The use of wikis is a convenient and practical way of accomplishing these tasks, because they can be implemented as depositories of collected information, which can later be organized, evaluated, and synthesized into intelligible research.

■ Critical Thinking and Problem Solving

Students must use critical thinking skills to plan and conduct research, solve problems, and make informed decisions using appropriate digital tools and resources. This means that students must learn to identify problems or form inquiries and organize an investigation to gather data to accomplish their task. It also implies that they utilize management skills to organize the information retrieved and develop it into a completed assignment.

While some students are natural problem-solvers, most students will need motivation to do the higher-level thinking required for evaluating and synthesizing information. Students' natural gravitation to the use of social networking technology may be the motivational key that will provide the peer interaction that encourages this critical thinking. Wikis are an extension of the new interactive technology that lays the foundation for higher-level thinking to occur, especially when wikis are utilized for collaboration between students.

Many people ask why wikis are so important in education and wonder whether typical Web pages would best serve the same purposes. The response to this is that, while Web pages serve to inform and communicate information, they are static entities. Perhaps the biggest obstacle to educators creating traditional Web pages is the fact that most educators do not have the training, skills, software, or time to make and maintain Web sites. Wikis, on the other hand, are interactive and easily edited, revised, and changed by the original author or—in some cases—another collaborator. A wiki is a set of hypertext linked documents, which is unique due to the fact that wiki users may edit the document, adding new sections and deleting or modifying old sections. To prevent defacement, most wikis have rules about who can edit and how they can edit. Wikis are easy to create, fast to put online, and simple to change if necessary. Moreover, teachers do not need advanced technology skills to create a wiki. Thus, educators and media specialists like the fact the wikis are easily created and offer collaborative properties that traditional Web pages lack.

As teachers, we endeavor to make learning uncomplicated and fun for our students. As media specialists, we strive to collaborate, make resources available to patrons, and help them navigate a wired, high-tech world. Wikis can be the vehicle to make these goals become reality, and they can do so for no cost, with no special technical skills, and without a huge investment of time. Wikis can be a lifeline in these difficult years, when standards and benchmarks drive education as we attempt to prepare students for futures that no one can yet envision. Wikis can bring structure to your world.

Three types of wikis that educators will find helpful are the library wiki, the reciprocal wiki, and the student-produced wiki.

The Library Wiki

A library wiki provides a storehouse for resources, information, documents, and audiovisual artifacts that the user collects for a particular purpose. It is usually locked down, or secured, so that users of the wiki cannot alter the information it contains; however, users can comment on the information.

One of the best uses for a library wiki is one that systematically lists information, resources, and directions for a student-centered alternative assessment project. The product of this type of project assignment can be anything from a formal research paper to an oral presentation, Power Point, podcast, or video production. The library wiki warehouses safe online resources; teacher-directed instructions; links to useful interactive sites; as well as images, video, audio, documents, or other materials that students may or may not need to complete a particular assignment. A library wiki becomes an online extension of the media specialist, as it leads students to relevant, safe, unbiased, and factual knowledge that they can analyze and synthesize into the final product. This type of direction is most useful to students who are just learning how to do research, how to cite sources, and how to use information they get without plagiarizing the source material.

Another use for the library wiki is for communication of school-based information for staff, because it can maintain a secure file of data that teachers and staff need to access on a regular basis. This type of wiki will become the place where teachers could find important information without searching files of e-mails or documents on their personal computers.

More information on the creation of and specific uses for the library wiki is found in chapter 5.

The Reciprocal Wiki

The reciprocal wiki is an online tool used by educators and media specialists to collaborate with classroom teachers, students, and parents. It is used primarily for organization and brainstorming. It can take the form of to-do lists, planning guides, curriculum plans, forecasting charts, or schedules. The purpose of this type of wiki is to enable diverse groups to work in partnership to achieve a common goal. They offer collaborative online storage space to create, revise, enhance and modify documents of all types and offer the choice of making the wiki a private (open just to designated individuals) or public (open to everyone) site.

The reciprocal wiki also offers an opportunity for sharing knowledge with a wider audience than one might encounter in normal day-to-day activities. At one time, ideas were shared in professional development workshops and staff meetings, but we now have a vehicle to accomplish the same purpose in less time, exerting less effort, and in an environment that elicits responses in a nonthreatening way.

More information on the development and creation of reciprocal wikis is found in chapter 6.

The Student-Produced Wiki

More than any other Web 2.0 tool or application, wikis represent access to total open content. This fact alone appeals to the 21st-century student, who texts, tweets, chats, and blogs on a daily basis. Online collaboration with other students and teachers is engaging to students, who quickly learn the procedural steps in wiki creation and usually are not afraid to experiment with the features wikis provide. This leads to exciting shared community conversation and development of documents and projects.

While the student-produced wiki is not a good vehicle for publishing, its real power is in the collaboration of developing, revising, and maintaining research, as well as sharing findings with a larger audience.

More information about motivating students and tips for wiki creation by students is found in chapter 7.

Examples of Educational Wikis

There are very good educational wikis online today. This book provides many real-world examples, but just to pique your interest, check out these exemplary models:

Booktalking with You A library wiki that contains a collection of book reviews and podcasts done by secondary students and categorized by genre. This wiki is an interesting collection of analyses of current books for young people. <http://booktalk.pbworks.com/>

Asalaamualiakum A student-produced wiki that is a collection of all of their research on the country of Pakistan. <http://asalaamualia kum.wikispaces.com/>

Litsource A reciprocal wiki where K–12 teachers can share lesson plans they recommend to teach reading. <https://litsource.wiki spaces.com/>

More examples follow, but you can see how wikis can enhance your classroom and make use of interactive Web 2.0 tools.

 THE SUPPORTING WIKI

It is only natural that I create a wiki that supports, enhances, and expands on the information found in this book. It will serve as an ongoing connection to readers, where the links in this printed book will be live and I can update the information frequently. More importantly, readers can post comments at this wiki site and can share new information with others. You can find my supporting wiki at: <http://educatorspowertool.pbworks.com>

Here is a chart to help you decide which type of wiki you are interested in using:

	WHAT DO YOU WANT TO ACCOMPLISH?	LIBRARY WIKI	RECIPROCAL WIKI	STUDENT-PRODUCED WIKI
A resource collection to organize student research	Make the best use of limited computer time for student research	X		
Collaborate with other educators in doing unit planning	Share ideas, resources, supplies, and suggestions		X	
Engage students in cooperative learning activities	Anytime communication for students working on joint assignments		X	X
Limit students to resources that are accurate, unbiased, and current	Resources are preselected	X		
Multistudent writing assignments	A medium for learning to edit and revise writing assignments		X	X
A resource collection for training teachers	Storehouse of professional development materials	X	X	
A tool for note-taking and mapping plans	Collaborative effort for planning		X	X

Figure 1.1. Checklist Organizer: Finding the Wiki To Fit the Need

The following chapters will help you produce the best possible wiki for your needs.

CHAPTER 2

What Is Collaboration?

Wikis are collaboration tools. The definition of collaboration is the act of working with one or more people in order to achieve something. Business has embraced collaboration between employees for years, creating teams to take on important projects, share knowledge, conceive ideas, and finish tasks in a specific time frame. Education, however, has been slow to embrace the concept of collaborative planning and teaching. I believe the reason for the breakdown in communication begins at the roots of U.S. education—the one-room schoolhouse.

In the one-room schoolhouse, one teacher was in charge of multiple grade levels with no one else to work in partnership with, share resources, or work together to solve everyday problems. Teachers were islands; they had to depend on their own educational background and what (typically meager) resources were available to teach several grade levels simultaneously. Often the only adult in the building, they took on not only teaching responsibilities but administrative, disciplinary, and custodial duties as well. They became very independent and relied on their own skill set to survive.

As education progressed in the 20th century to large, multiclassroom buildings, teachers carried a lot of that autonomous professional personality into that new setting. They might have shared a common hallway, but they closed their doors and taught in their own worlds using their tried-and-true skill set to accomplish the task of teaching students. Someone once described this as the "egg-carton effect," where all the eggs reside in the same Styrofoam carton and are treated as one entity, but in reality never touch each other.

My Personal Experience

When I began my teaching career in 1970, this egg-carton environment was prevalent. I had noticed that one of my colleagues was gearing up for a special project of creating framed silhouettes of each child in her class to send home for a terrific Mother's Day present. It was a great idea, and I thought my students needed to bring home silhouettes also. When my colleague found out I was collecting resources for the project, she told me directly that this was her initiative and no one else could copy her idea or use her project—ever. It was a life lesson for me at the time: Success depended on your personal creativity and resources to achieve. I quickly retreated into my section of the egg carton with apologies to my colleague. I went to work my second year and created the most elaborate Chinese New Year celebration the community had ever seen—complete with Chinese lanterns, a papier-mâché dragon head winding through the hallways with the entire class under dyed sheets following behind, and a sophisticated Chinese luncheon for parents. It was dynamite! Moreover, it was mine! I received accolades from administration and parents, and even my colleague who took exception with me doing silhouettes gave me her approval. I had arrived at the apex of success in the egg-carton school environment. Moreover, for seven years, I thought that because I embraced the norm of that setting, I was successful.

A few years later and when I went on to become a media specialist, I began to think how sad it was that all the professionals in our school lived in separate spheres, utilizing their energies singularly. This individual energy, when combined with the energy of other professionals, would be an amalgamation of many skills, resources, and ideas that would result in a synergy that would far outpace what any single classroom teacher could accomplish alone. I was not alone in this realization, because at about this same time came the advent of collaboration in educational settings.

Collaboration was not an easy sell to veteran teachers, who were satisfied with the status quo. New teachers, however, embraced the concept fully, and as the years went by, collaboration of faculty with their colleagues in most school settings was accepted and expected. Educational research has confirmed the importance of collaboration to the professional development of educators. Research tells us that collaboration brings many rewards to teachers:

- Through formal and informal training sessions, study groups, and conversations about teaching, teachers and administrators gain the opportunity to get smarter together.

- Teachers are better prepared to support one another's strengths and accommodate weaknesses. Working together, they reduce their individual planning time while greatly increasing the available pool of ideas and materials.

- Schools become better prepared and organized to examine new ideas, methods, and materials. The faculty becomes adaptable and self-reliant.

- Teachers are organized to ease the strain of staff turnover, both by providing systematic professional assistance to beginners and by explicitly socializing all newcomers, including veteran teachers, to staff values, traditions, and resources (Inger, 1993).

Collaboration Today

Fast forward to the present, and we find that collaboration among educational professionals is still a relevant and productive model. As a media specialist and 40-year veteran educator, I have access to both tactics and knowledge that I willingly share with my colleagues on a daily basis. However, I have witnessed another upheaval to the educational system that threatens the collaborative environment. Education has become standards based, with high-stakes testing setting the goals of many school districts. Curriculum maps leave little room for creative teaching. The depressed economy has burdened the structure of schools with fewer resources and less planning time allotted for teacher preparation. The result has been that teachers collaborate to a lesser extent in the data-driven environment. School sites that once encouraged and rewarded collaborative sharing of strategies and ideas and a culture of teamwork have buckled under to the restraints of operating schools in a depressed economy.

State standards, curriculum mapping, and district edicts about lesson planning and specific teaching strategies now drive schools, and innovation and collaboration have almost disappeared. However, today's teachers realize that their jobs have become more difficult and stressful without the collaborative environment to which they have become accustomed. A review of education literature finds that teachers in many schools still feel isolated. More often than not, they have no formal opportunities to collaborate. It is even rarer for teachers with busy schedules, too many classes, and too many students to take the time independently to collaborate formally with colleagues (Kohm &

Nance, 2009). This results in problematic symptoms of a toxic school environment:

- **Lack of shared meaning** A teacher will suggest something to a colleague using a term or phrase whose meaning is different for the listener. Although the listener believes she is responding to the comment or question, the meanings of their words do not line up and the problem solving does not go forward.

- **Lack of shared conception of teaching role** A teacher brings up a problem, and a colleague responds by invoking a possible solution that requires something more or different of the teacher than he feels obligated to do. The solution is thus not viable for the teacher, and the conversation does not progress.

- **Lack of trust** A teacher makes a suggestion to a colleague about solving a problem of practice. The suggestion is rejected because the teacher reads an implicitly negative judgment from her colleague or believes that her colleague does not adequately appreciate the particularities of her problem (Horn, 2009).

Because collaboration is not as easy to accomplish as it once was, this does not mean its importance has diminished. Current research has demonstrated that collaboration among teachers has a positive effect on high-stakes test scores. In one study, the researchers wanted to determine the relationship between teacher collaboration and student achievement. They used reading and math achievement scores for 2,536 fourth-graders, controlling for school context and student characteristics such as prior achievement. They found a positive relationship between teacher collaboration and differences among schools in mathematics and reading achievement (McClure, 2009).

To foster this positive school culture, educators must now devise methods to continue sharing information in response to the difficult circumstances that consume their working day. Using the tools inherent to Web 2.0 technology is a way educators can continue to build working relationships with other professionals beyond the limits of social exchanges found in texting, chatting, or blogging. The technology best fitting the challenge of collaborating online is the wiki.

Wikis allow multiple collaborators and can ensure that no one is in control of the process. In minutes, teachers can create a workable wiki. From any Internet browser at any time, teachers can edit the wiki in seconds. The wiki centers on communication of ideas and not the technology itself. The wiki tool affords the advantage of reducing the technical skill required to use its features, allowing users to focus on the information exchange and collaborative tasks themselves without the distraction of a difficult technological environment. In addition, because the nature of the collaborative information is not confidential, it can be accessed by other educational professionals beyond one school's walls to allow even more vision into a project.

Wikis facilitate teachers to become authors and editors of content, plans, goals, ideas, and resources within a community. Attempts at school improvement cannot be individual and fragmented, but rather must be embedded in collaborative practices that address the day-to-day needs of students (Leonard & Leonard, 2009). The future may see wikis as the primary vehicle of professional collaboration, because wikis can be used in a variety of ways. Teachers who see value in collaboration will use wikis as a strategy to communicate, share, and find consensus in their methods—ultimately making the difficult job of teaching a little less stressful. Wikis are a communicative medium that assists teachers in an important aspect of their job. Wikis are indeed a powerful and useful tool.

Once teachers feel comfortable with using wikis as a vehicle for collaboration, they have a better understanding of the need for collaboration in student work as well. By collaborating, students can develop their potential for learning. Students and teachers alike participate in collaborative communication of content and beyond. Specifically, students can learn to approach and solve new problems so that they develop the capability to solve problems that do not exist at the moment of learning. Rather than simply absorbing material, learning rules, and displaying the material and rules on demand, students learn to develop capabilities that they first experience in assisted or collaborative learning situations (Enabling Student Collaboration for Learning, 2009). Student collaboration encourages higher-level-thinking strategies and online collaboration that utilizes Web 2.0 technology, that most students already have embraced, facilitates a comfort zone for that collaboration to take place. Wikis enhance asynchronous communication and cooperative learning among students, and promote cooperation rather than competition (Parker & Chao, 2007).

By incorporating wikis into the school workplace, educators can better prepare students to make innovative uses of collaborative software tools and collaborate with their peers. These are the skills valued by the business community as key innovations in the business practices of today and in the future. Today's students will not only participate in collaborative technology in their careers, they will be the force behind them. As educators, we need to prepare our students both in collaborative skills and in the social networking tools that support collaboration.

The centerpiece of wiki use is collaboration, whether students implement wikis for research projects or teachers use wikis for professional development purposes. We can no longer ignore the importance of collaboration in today's world, where management of the overwhelming amount of information has become a prerequisite for learning. Wikis provide a stage for teachers to demonstrate their knowledge, strategies, and ideas that would otherwise go unnoticed if they were to operate in the lonely environment of their classrooms. The advantage of sharing, whether it is among colleagues or student-to-student sharing, can only serve to strengthen education for everyone.

CHAPTER 3

The ABCs of Producing a Wiki

Setting up a wiki is a simple process. Writing out the directions for doing so makes the task look much more daunting than it actually is. Do not be put off by the length of this explanation, because it takes many words to describe an action that in reality takes a one-second click of the mouse. However, it is essential to have a guide that explains each step in detail for your future reference.

Envision Your Wiki

Before you begin creating your wiki, you will want to have a clear vision of the purpose of your wiki workspace. These questions may help with envisioning your wiki purpose:

- Will your wiki be a temporary workspace, or will you be using it on a more permanent basis?

- Will your wiki be accessible to others in order for collaboration to occur, or will you want to use the site as a warehouse of resources and will want to limit editing capabilities?

- Will you want to embed media such as audio or video files in your wiki?

- Will your front page be a table of contents with links to subsequent pages of content?

- Will your wiki be primarily text based, or will you want to enhance its look with interactive posters or text clouds (see chapter 4)?

- Will you include widgets or gadgets in your wiki (see chapter 4)?
- Will you be adding graphics to your wiki workspace?

Choosing a Host Site for Your Wiki

There are several host sites to choose from to create a wiki. Some of the most popular are:

Google Sites
<http://www.google.com/sites/help/intl/en/overview.html#>

Google has created an easy site to generate a wiki that includes templates for common purposes. The classroom template will provide an easy way for you to communicate with parents and the community.

Wikidot
<http://www.wikidot.com/more:explore-features>

This site allows you create up to five wikis with a maximum of 400 megabytes of storage in each. Other features include the creation of your own personal avatar that will appear on your page and favicons (icons of your wiki that show up on the title bar of your browser).

Wetpaint
<http://www.wetpaint.com/page/Wetpaint-Features>

Wetpaint is a slick site that specializes in social wikis with many contributors. It provides templates for beginners.

Wikispaces
<http://www.wikispaces.com/site/features>

Wikispaces is one of the most popular wiki hosting sites among educators and offers two gigabytes of file storage at no cost.

PBworks
<http://pbworks.com/academictour>

PBworks is another popular host site among educators. It offers themed pages and two gigabytes of file storage. It is a simple-to-use site that offers many useful reporting strategies.

All of these sites are powerful tools, and all of them use the same what-you-see-is-what-you-get creative tools. For the purposes of this explanation, I have chosen PBworks to walk you through the process. The directions are similar for all of the host sites listed.

Setting Up a Wiki

1. Go to <https://plans.pbworks.com/academic#> and click on the free basic classroom wiki button at the lower right-hand side of the page.

2. A pop-up window will ask if you want to upgrade to a premium wiki that will give you more storage and a few extra features. If you are just beginning to use this technology, you will probably not be interested in this option, and you can always upgrade later. Click on:

   No thanks—just create my Basic Edition workspace.

3. At this point, you must create a title for your wiki. Enter a name in the text field and it will complete the URL for your wiki. This URL will be the Web address where people will be able to access your wiki once it is completed.

4. Under the section labeled **Agree to non-commercial use,** choose **For education** and check the box to agree that the wiki is to be used for non-commercial use only.

5. Click the **NEXT** button in the lower right-hand corner of the page.

6. On the next page, you will see two questions. The first question is **Who can view this workspace?** The default is **Anyone**, and you should leave this response, unless you want to keep the wiki private until you finish working on it. You can always change this option later.

7. The next question is **Who can edit this workspace?** The default is **Only people I invite or approve**, and, again, you should leave this default response.

8. Click the box to agree to the PBworks terms of service.

9. Check the box at the bottom of the page that you agree to the terms of service and click on the **Take Me to My Workspace** button at the bottom of the page.

10. Your new wiki will open with some placeholder text already added to the wiki's first page. The **Front Page**, which is the name for the first page of your wiki, you will edit to reflect your own content.

Before attempting to add content to your wiki, you will want to familiarize yourself with the management features. Once you have set up a wiki, you can assign permissions that will determine the level of access visitors to the wiki site will have:

- *Administrator* You will assume the role of administrator because you are the wiki's creator and owner. This assignment occurs automatically. This role allows you to add and remove users, change permissions, and access the settings page.

- *Editor* Editors can rename and delete pages, files, and folders of the wiki. You need to be cautious in assigning this role, because it allows the removal of content from the wiki and there is a threat of wiki sabotage implicit in this role.

- *Writer* A writer can edit pages and revert them to previous versions of the pages. You will assign the role of writer to the majority of people who you invite to use the wiki.

- *Reader* A reader can only view content on the wiki and does not have the ability to edit or make any changes.

Assigning User Roles

1. Click on the **Settings** tab at the top of your wiki's front page, and the settings page for your wiki will open up.

2. Under **Access Controls** in the middle of the left-hand column, click on **Users**.

3. On this page, you can enter the e-mail addresses of each user you want to add, select the role you want to assign to them from the pull-down menu, and click on **Add User**. This will send an invitation e-mail to each user with a link to access the wiki.

If you want to assign user roles to students who do not have their own e-mail accounts, PBworks has made user names and passwords available for the administrator (teacher) to assign to students in order for them to be editors of the wiki site.

Adding and Formatting Content

You may edit the content on the wiki page if you assume the role of administrator, editor, or writer (you may have to log in and provide the wiki password/invite key first). To edit, follow these directions:

1. Click on the **Edit** tab at the top of the front page.

2. On the front page, you will see some placeholder text. Select the placeholder text and press the **Delete** key on your keyboard to remove it and replace it with your own text. On other new pages you create, you will start out with a blank page.

3. Once you have entered your text, use the buttons at the top of the page to edit.

   - You can make the text bold, italic, or underlined by selecting the text you want to stylize and click on the appropriate button in the toolbar:

   B <u>U</u> *I*

- To add a list, click on the bottom for the type of list you want to add (ordered or bulleted) and begin typing the text for the first list item. To add more list items, press the **Enter** key or **Return** key on the keyboard. When your list is finished, click on the list button in the toolbar one more time.

- To indent text, place the cursor at the beginning of the line you wish to indent, and then click on the **Increase Indent** button on the toolbar. To undo the indentation, click on the **Decrease Indent** button.

- To change the alignment, click on the left, center, or right align button in the toolbar.

- To change the text or background color, click on the appropriate color button and select a color swatch from the pull-down menu.

- To change the font or text size, elect the text you want to format and select a different font or text size using the pull-down menus in the toolbar.

- To add a heading, select the text you want to use as the heading and select a heading level (Heading 1 to Heading 6) from the **Format** pull-down menu.

- To remove all formatting, select the text from which you want to remove all formatting and click on the **Remove Formatting** button.

- To undo the last edit, click on the **Undo** button on the toolbar.

- To add a horizontal rule to divide sections of text, place the cursor on a blank line and click on the **Insert Horizontal Rule** button.

- To enter any tags (or keywords) you want to be associated with your page, add them in the **Tags** field at the bottom of the page.

- Click on the **SAVE** button when you are done with all of your editing.

Changing Wiki Settings

To inspect the settings for your wiki, click on the **Settings** tab at the top of any of the wiki's pages. Free accounts do not allow modifications of all settings. Here is a list of the ones you can modify:

- *About This Space* This setting allows you to change the title text that appears at the top of each page, enter a brief description of the wiki's contents, and change the contact e-mail of the wiki's administrator.

- *Logo* This option allows you to use a photo or other image as a logo at the top of every wiki page. Click on **Browse** and locate the image you wish to use, then click on **Upload Logo**. You can choose to have the wiki's colors change to reflect the colors in your logo image, or you can choose your own color scheme. This is a good feature for adding a school mascot to your wiki.

- *Colors* Here you can select a color scheme for your wiki. The color schemes available in a free account are limited to nine basic options. To customize the color scheme, you will need to upgrade to a premium account.

- *Workspace Security* This option allows you to determine whether a wiki will be private or public. Checking the box next to **Let users request permission** allows you to add users upon their request. As the administrator of the wiki, you will see **Pending user requests** listed at the top of the **Users** page in the wiki's settings. Also at this section, you can choose to disable all reader comments on the wiki.

- *Delete* This option allows the administrator of the wiki to delete the workspace completely. This action permanently deletes the wiki, so be sure you no longer want to use it before initiating this action. Even the wiki name is permanently deleted and can never be used again.

- *Back-up* This option allows you to backup all wiki pages but only if you have purchased a premium workspace.

Uploading Files

Up to two gigabytes of files can be uploaded to a PBworks site in a free account. To upload a file:

1. Click on **Upload/view files** at the top of any wiki page.

2. Click on the **Browse** button and locate the file you want to upload to the wiki site.

3. Click on the link for **Upload**. A list of uploaded files will appear at the bottom of the screen.

4. To rename a file you have uploaded, click on **Rename**, and enter a new name in the text field.

5. To remove an uploaded file from the wiki, click on the box to the left of the file name, then click on the **Delete** button at the top of the page.

Adding Images

To add an image to a wiki page, you must first upload the image file:

1. Open the wiki page for editing.

2. Click on the tab for **Pages and Files**, located on the top of the page.

3. Click on Upload files button and locate the image file on your computer.

4. Click on **Open,** and your image file will be uploaded.

Once you upload the image file, place the cursor where you want to add the image on the page and click on the image in the **Images and Files** list. To resize the image, drag on the handles that appear when you select it on the wiki page.

Creating Hyperlinks

To add a link on a wiki page:

1. Select the text you want to turn into a link.

2. Click on the **Add Link** button in the toolbar.

3. Select the **Link Type** at the top of the **Insert Link** pull-down window:

   - *Wiki Page* Select the page you want to link using the **Page** pull-down menu.

   - *PBwiki Folder/File* Select a file or folder using the **Folder or File** pull-down menu.

   - *Web Page* Select **URL** as the link type, choose **http** as the protocol, and enter the address of the page in the URL field.

   - *Email* Enter the e-mail address in the field at the bottom of the pop-up window.

4. Click on **OK** to add the link to the page. If you need to edit the link, select the link text and click on the **Insert/Edit Link** button. This will open the **Insert Link** pop-up window, where you can make changes.

A quick way to add a link to another wiki page on a wiki site is by selecting the link text and clicking on the page you want to link to in the **Images and Files** list that appears to the right of every wiki page.

Inserting a Table

You can use columns to align text with a table. To add a table to any PBworks page:

1. Place the cursor where you want to insert the table.

2. Click on the **Add Table** button in the toolbar.

3. Enter the number of columns and rows and the table width.

4. Click on **OK** once you have set all of the table options to add the table to the wiki page. When you right-click (or **Control-click** for Mac) on a table, you will see the following options:

- *Cell* Allows you to add, remove, and split cells. Choose **Cell Properties** to access more properties such as word wrapping, vertical and horizontal alignment of cell contents, and background and border colors.

- *Row* Here you can add and remove rows.

- *Column* This option allows you to add and remove columns.

- *Delete table* Here you can remove the table from the page.

- *Table Properties* This option opens the same properties as when you click on the **Add Table** button in the toolbar.

Adding and Managing Pages

You can add multiple pages to your wiki, thus creating a wiki site. To add a page:

1. Under the **Pages** tab of the **Insert Links** menu located on the right-hand side of the wiki page, click on **Insert a Link to a New Page**.

2. Enter a name for the new page in the text field at the top of the screen.

3. Click on **No Template** to create a blank page, or select one of the available templates to create a page with some content already inserted.

4. Click on **Create New Page** and begin editing the new page. Make sure to click on **SAVE** when you are finished to add the page to the wiki site.

To view all the pages on your site, click on the **View All Pages** link on the right side of any wiki page. This will display a list of all the pages along with the time and date of the last revision and the e-mail address of the person who made the revision.

To remove a page from the site, click on the **Remove** button to the right of the pages list and click on **OK** to confirm that you really want to remove the page. To rename a page, click on the **Rename** button, enter the new name, and click on **Rename** again.

The Sidebar is a special page on your wiki site that appears embedded on the right side of every other page. You can add navigation for your wiki on the Sidebar by placing links to all the other pages on the wiki site. Click on the **Edit the Sidebar** link at the bottom of the Sidebar to open it for editing just as you would any other page.

Organizing Wiki Site Files

As your wiki site grows, you may find it helpful to organize the pages and other files into folders, just as you probably organize files on your computer. To create a new folder on your wiki site, look under the **Pages and Files** link on the right-hand side of any wiki page and click on the **Create a Folder** link.

To place a page in a folder, drag the file you select into the folder you have created.

To remove a page from a folder, open the folder and click on the individual file you wish to delete. Then click on the **Delete** button at the top of the page.

Revisions

PBworks keeps track of every change you make to the wiki to make it easy to go back to a previous version if you make a mistake. To view the most recent activity on the entire wiki, scroll down the page until you see the **Recent Wiki Activity** section. This section will display the most recent changes made to the wiki.

To view a list of all revisions for a page, first click on **View all pages** on the right side of the screen, and then click on the link under **Revisions** for the page you wish to review. Next, click on the date and time of the revision you wish to view. This will open the page as it appeared at that time. To save this version of the page, click on **Revert to this version** at the top of the screen. To return to the most recent version of the page, click on the **View current version** link.

In the **View all pages** screen, you can delete individual revisions by clicking on the red **Delete** button to the right of each revision. You can also compare two revisions by selecting with the radio buttons on the left and clicking on the **Compare** button. To make it easier to tell them apart, the two revisions will be displayed in different text colors.

Extending Wikis with Plug-ins

You can use PBworks plug-ins to add videos, slide shows, calendars, and more. To add a plug-in to a PBworks page:

1. Place the cursor where you want to add the plug-in on the page.
2. Click on the **Insert Plugin** button in the toolbar. This will open the **Insert Plugin** pop-up window.

3. Click on a category to see the plug-ins available under that category.

4. Click on the link for the plug-in you wish to add to your page.

5. The remaining steps for adding the plug-in will vary depending on the plug-in chosen, but you should see a **Preview** button that will allow you to preview how the plug-in will appear on the page before you insert it. If you are happy with the results, click on **OK** to add the plug-in to the page.

To resize a plug-in once you have added it to the page, drag on the handles that appear when you select it.

Sharing a Wiki

In addition to inviting other people to become users, there are two other ways you can share a wiki:

- Using the wiki's RSS feed. (RSS is the format for distributing news and other Web content. When you put content into RSS and send that content to other people or Web sites, it's called a feed.)

- Sharing the print version of a wiki page.

By subscribing to the RSS feed for a wiki, other people can track the latest updates to the wiki. To view the RSS feed for the wiki, click on the RSS feed link at the bottom of the page. The RSS feed will display correctly, if you are accessing it with a Web browser that can read RSS feeds. To share the RSS feed, copy the URL in the browser's Web address field and paste it into an e-mail or add it to your Web site.

To save a print version of any wiki page, click on the **Printable version** link at the bottom of the page. This will open a ready-to-print version of the page in your Web browser without all of the PBworks buttons and links that normally appear on the right side and at the bottom of the screen.

Adding Tags

Every page in PBworks can have several tags associated with it. To find a page when you cannot remember the exact title of the page, use tags, which are similar to keywords. To add a tag to a page, click on the **Add Tags** link found on the right side of the screen. You can add multiple tags by separating them with a comma.

When you search PBworks using a tag, type the word *tag* followed by a colon and the name of the tag. For example, to search a PBworks site for all pages tagged with the word *geography,* you would type **tag: geography**.

When you have created your first wiki, you may think it looks uninteresting—even drab. There are things you can do to make the wiki more appealing and elicit plenty of student interest. You may also feel that the wiki is a great tool but lacks the security you want to safeguard your documents against tampering or vandalism. The next chapter addresses both of these concerns with items you can include in your wiki to both dress up and button down the look of your design.

CHAPTER 4

Dressing Up and Buttoning Down Your Wiki

Making Wikis More Engaging

When your wiki is complete, it is essentially a text-based Web page. Any experienced teacher can tell you that students do not engage as well with text-based content as they do when the information is dressed up with graphics. Clip art, photos, and graphs and charts will help make your wiki more useable and will create more interest among your students. You can add clip art and photos that enhance your wiki page with your own creations (uploaded as files and inserted in the wiki), or you can use free clip art and photos from Internet sites. It is important to consider copyright provisions when looking for photos and clip art and only to use sites that offer copyright-free images. Some sites that offer copyright-free material are:

Google Clipart

<http://images.google.com/images?hl=en&um=1&sa=1&q=clipart&bt nG=Search&aq=f&oq=&aqi=g10&start=0> Searchable by topic.

Google Photos

<http://images.google.com/images?hl=en&um=1&sa=1&q=photo&btn G=Search> Searchable by topic.

Iclipart.com

<http://free-clipart.net/> Includes animated graphics.

Barry's Clipart Server

<http://www.barrysclipart.com/> Organized by topic.

Adding Widgets, Gadgets, and Tools

A widget is a stand-alone application that can be embedded into a PB-works site by an administrator or editor of the PBworks site. Servers other than the original host site, enabling dynamic content that will enhance your wiki site, often serve the various contents of widgets. Some common widgets include weather guides, stock lists, flight trackers, calendars, and search boxes for various Web sites.

There are many places to find widgets on the Internet. Some of the most popular sites are:

Google Gadgets for Your Webpage <http://www.google.com/ig/ directory?synd=open>

Google has listed more than 180,000 widgets (which it calls Gadgets), and these are searchable by category (Tools, Games, Technology, etc.).

Widgetbox <http://www.widgetbox.com/>

This site has made 175,000 widgets available, and these can be searched by tag name.

Bravenet Website Widgets <http://www.bravenet.com/webtools/wid gets.php>

This site has talking character widgets that can be added to your page.

Yahoo Widget Page <http://widgets.yahoo.com/>

Yahoo has created a site with thousands of widgets and a tab that allows you to create your own widget.

Once you have chosen a suitable widget for your page, you will need to install it on your wiki site:

1. Copy the source HTML code from the widget you select.

2. In the editing mode on your PBworks page, place the cursor at the location you wish to add the widget.

3. Click on the **Insert Plug-in** tab at the top of the page.

4. Click on **HTML & Gadgets**.

5. On the drop-down menu, select **HTML/Javascript**.

6. In the empty box, paste the source code you copied from the widget site.

TYPE OF PLUG-IN	DIRECTIONS FOR INSERTING PLUG-IN	DESCRIPTION
Video	<https://educators.pbworks.com/video>	Embed an existing video from any video hosting site.
Screencast	<https://educators.pbworks.com/screencast>	Create tutorials and post them on your workspace.
Avatar	<https://educators.pbworks.com/avatar>	Add character to your online personality.
Poster	<https://educators.pbworks.com/glogster>	Build an interactive poster with video, audio, and text.
Wordle	<https://educators.pbworks.com/wordle>	Create word clouds
Voice thread	<https://educators.pbworks.com/Voicethread>	Develop a spoken narrative to photos.
Surveys and polls	<https://educators.pbworks.com/polls>	Create a poll or survey and embed it on your workspace.
Chat	<https://educators.pbworks.com/chat>	Real-time chat on your workspace.
Footnotes and equations	<https://educators.pbworks.com/footnotes>	Easy-to-use plug-ins that help develop good digital citizenship.
PowerPoint presentation	<https://educators.pbworks.com/presentation>	Upload or embed existing PowerPoint presentations so they are accessible from anywhere.
Twitter4Teachers	<http://twitter4teachers.pbworks.com/>	Find other teachers on Twitter (links to an external site).

Figure 4.1. PBworks: Make It Easy To Use Plug-ins

7. Click the box next to the words: **Allow Javascript and potentially unsafe code** (this is important if Javascript is included in the code).

8. Click on the **Preview** button.

9. Click on **OK**.

Another interesting effect that can be incorporated into a wiki page is the addition of cloud text. For this dramatic effect, you can generate a cloud of text from the following sites and insert it into a wiki page using the on-screen generator instructions:

Text Tag Cloud Generator <http://www.artviper.net/texttagcloud/>

TagCrowd <http://tagcrowd.com/>

Wordle <http://www.wordle.net/>

To view the use of cloud text in a wiki, check out this site:

eSandbox <http://esandbox.wikispaces.com/>

To take the wiki to a new level of graphics, you can use Glogster to make an interactive page on the wiki.

Glogster <http://www.glogster.com>

This site will turn your wiki page into a poster. You can use the simple drag-and-drop graphics and labels to enhance your wiki page. You will need to link your labels to other wiki pages before you save your Glogster creation. Then you can copy the source code and paste it into the wiki using the plug-in instructions detailed earlier in this chapter. The result is a wiki page that is inviting, exciting, and engaging.

Here are some models of wiki pages that use Glogster to enhance the page:

Bookleads <http://bookleads.wikispaces.com/>

New Tools Workshop <http://newtoolsworkshop.wikispaces.com/>

Another creative way to enhance a wiki is to use speaking avatars. Avatars are animated cartoon creations that will speak the words you record in your own voice. The service is free and is an easy drag-and-drop interface. You can make your avatar at the Voki site: <http://www.voki.com/>

To enhance your wiki using an avatar, log on to the Voki Web site, and then follow these directions:

1. Click **Create**.

2. Create your Voki character with a unique, appropriate message.

3. Click **Publish**.

4. Copy the HTML code.

5. Log in to your wiki and navigate to the page where you want your avatar to appear.

6. Click **Edit** at the top of the page. Be sure you are editing the right page!

7. Click Plugin. Paste the HTML code you copied in step 4.

8. Click **Preview**, then click **Save**.

Examples of wikis that use this enhancement can be found at the following sites:

Wee Web Wonders <http://weewebwonders.synthasite.com/voki.php>

ABC ICT <http://abcict.wikispaces.com/>

As you become more expert at creating wikis, you may want to add effects such as pop-ups, logos, rollovers, text effects, or you may want to insert maps or Google Earth screens. Here is a list of some of the more popular add-ons to wikis:

WIDGET/GADGET/ TOOL FUNCTION	WHERE TO GET IT
Arabic Word of the Day	<http://www.widgetbox.com/widget/arabic-audio-word-of-the-day>
Atomic Clock	<http://www.widgetbox.com/widget/atomic-clock>
Body Mass Index Calculator	<http://www.widgetbox.com/widget/bmi>
Breast Cancer Support	<http://www.widgetbox.com/widget/breast-cancer-support>
Butterfly Clock	<http://www.springwidgets.com/widgets/view/56926>
Button Generator	<http://www.buttongenerator.com/>
Calculator	<http://www.widgetbox.com/widget/calculator-gwidget>
Calorie Counter	<http://www.widgetbox.com/widget/calorie-calculator>
Chinese Word of the Day	<http://www.widgetbox.com/widget/chinese-audio-word-of-the-day>
Christmas Tree	<http://www.springwidgets.com/widgets/view/46>
Daily Horoscope	<http://www.google.com/ig/directory?synd=open&url=http://www.google.com/ig/modules/horoscope.xml>
Earth Day	<http://www.springwidgets.com/widgets/view/31141>
Eiffel Tower Live WebCam	<http://www.google.com/ig/directory?synd=open&url=http://www.paris-live.com/module/module.xml>

Figure 4.2. Where To Find Widgets and Gadgets

WIDGET/GADGET/ TOOL FUNCTION	WHERE TO GET IT
Feed the Fish	<http://www.google.com/ig/ directory?synd=open&url=http://fishgadget.google code.com/svn/trunk/fish.xml>
French Word of the Day	<http://www.widgetbox.com/widget/french-audio-word-of-the-day>
Glitter Text Generator	<http://www.glittertools.com/28/glitters.html>
Google Search Tool	<http://www.widgetbox.com/widget/google-search-tool>
Grade Point Average Calculator	<http://www.widgetbox.com/widget/gpa-calculator>
Grammar Girl Quiz	<http://www.widgetbox.com/widget/grammargirlquiz>
How Stuff Works	<http://www.widgetbox.com/widget/hsw-search>
Japanese Word of the Day	<http://www.widgetbox.com/widget/japanese-word-of-the-day>
Joke of the Day	<http://www.google.com/ig/directory? synd=open&url=http://sortr.com/jokes/joke.xml>
Latest Front Pages from around the World	<http://www.widgetbox.com/widget/latest-front-page-from-around-the-world>
Math Man	<http://www.widgetbox.com/widget/math-man>
Maukie: The Virtual Cat	<http://www.google.com/ig/directory?synd=open&hl= en&gl=en&url=http://www.atlas-labs.net/gadgets/wid get/virtualcat/virtualcat.xml>
News on Sciencentral	<http://www.widgetbox.com/widget/new-on-sciencentral>
Quake Shake	<http://www.widgetbox.com/widget/whats-shaking>
Random Daily History Quotes	<http://www.widgetbox.com/widget/daily-history-quote>
Rhyme Dictionary	<http://www.widgetbox.com/widget/rhyme-dictionary>
Russian Word of the Day	<http://www.widgetbox.com/widget/russian-audio-word-of-the-day>
Save the Earth Quiz	<http://www.widgetbox.com/widget/save-the-earth-quiz-add-to-it-share-it>
Space in 3D	<http://www.widgetbox.com/widget/solar-system-in-3d>
Spanish Word of the Day	<http://www.widgetbox.com/widget/spanish-word-of-the-day-declan>
State Animals	<http://www.widgetbox.com/widget/state-animals>

Figure 4.2. (*Continued*)

WIDGET/GADGET/ TOOL FUNCTION	WHERE TO GET IT
Text Effects Tools	<http://www.glittertools.com/5/text-effects.html>
This Day in History	<http://www.widgetbox.com/widget/this-day-in-history-cdouthard>
Timeline of U.S. Presidents	<http://www.widgetbox.com/widget/timeline-us-presidents>
Unit Converter	<http://www.widgetbox.com/widget/unit-converter>
USA Smarts	<http://www.widgetbox.com/widget/usa-smarts>
Weather Channel	<http://www.yourminis.com/minis/yourminis/antwean/mini:45>
Word Art	<http://www.widgetbox.com/widget/word-art-by-abrakadoodle>
Word of the Day	<http://www.widgetbox.com/widget/shrivastavaaditya>

Figure 4.2. (*Continued*)

One of the best resources for instructions on how to make these enhancements and thousands of other add-ons can be found at this site:

Getting Tricky with Wikis <http://gettingtrickywithwikis.wikispaces.com/>

Basic wikis are easy to create, easy to edit, and easy to use. As you work with wikis, you will probably find a template that you find works for you and your classroom. The enhancements are just a fun way to impact student engagement with the content.

Securing Your Wiki

Like other Web 2.0 tools, security issues may occur with wikis. Wikis have a safeguard built in to restrict usage and limit access of certain users while allowing other users to edit. **Hidden** pages are wiki pages that allows you to create private content that you do not want to share with others or pages you are working on and are not yet ready to share with all users. **Lockable** pages allow you to create wiki pages that no other user can edit. This comes in handy if you are putting student assignments on a wiki, and you do not want students editing the content.

How To Hide and Lock Pages

1. Log in to your wiki.

2. On the right-hand side of the workspace are three options:

   - Put this page in a folder
   - Add tags
   - Page security

3. Choose **Page security**.

4. Choose to **Hide** or **Lock** the page.

Another security feature is e-mail notifications. When the page is edited or modified, wikis have the ability to track every edit made to the workspace and send out notifications to the administrator (you). This option sends you an alert if you have students who are corrupting pages and gives you the opportunity to revert the content to its original format. To receive e-mail notifications of changes:

1. Go to My.PBworks.com.

2. Scroll down the page to the **Preferences** box, and change your notification settings.

One of the best features of the wiki is that it automatically saves every edit made to a workspace. This means that you can always check to see who edited the page and what time it was changed. If students accidentally delete content, change content, or upload inappropriate content, you will immediately be able to know who did it and when he or she did it, and you can reverse the changes. To access this feature:

1. Log in to your wiki.

2. Click on the link for **Page History** on the top of the page. Here you can compare edits and change back to a previous version if necessary.

Once you have added these extra security features to your original choice of who you allowed editing privileges, your wiki operation is as secure as any interactive site on the Internet.

CHAPTER 5

The Library Wiki

One of the best uses of wikis is as a library of resources for its users. This warehousing of sources, sites, media, and information has many purposes. It can serve as a repository of tools for teachers, students, or others. It can store instructions, rubrics, and resources for students to use in completing class projects. Teachers can use a library wiki to list their syllabus, complete with handouts, assignments, and special instructions for students. It can be used to inform, advertise, communicate, and report. The beauty of a library wiki is its ability to store documents and assignments that can be downloaded for completion from remote locations. Editing makes changes to schedules and plans simple and fast. Library wikis are powerful tools for teachers and media specialists.

For example, as a media specialist in a middle school setting, I know that the two of the most prevalent problems teachers face in assigning research projects are trying to make the most of precious computer lab time and keeping students organized and on-task during the research process.

1. Teachers know that online resources give their students unprecedented access to primary source materials that they can use in their research. The exceptional qualities of these resources are something students need to learn how to access, understand, and use to form reports or complete alternative projects. Yet when middle school students are placed in front of a computer and they begin the research search, they tend to end up at completely unrelated sites. They cannot explain how it happened—but the frequency of its occurrence is probably no accident. To prevent this off-task behavior and to make the most of precious computer lab time at most schools, wikis can store Web sites where students can directly access the information needed to complete an assignment.

2. Teachers spend time outlining the procedures, writing out written explanations, and verbalizing directions for student research assignments. Yet many students arrive at the computer lab or at home with little or no comprehension of how to do the assigned work. Today's students might be the best multitaskers ever produced, but few are well organized. Teachers and media specialists can use wikis to post systematic directions that can be easily accessed by students, parents, and special teachers to aid students in finishing the project assigned.

The following chart describes some of the most popular uses for library wikis:

LIBRARY WIKI RESOURCE	VALUE TO EDUCATOR
Storehouse of pertinent Web sites	Keeps students focused on assignment and directs them to accurate, unbiased information.
Warehouse of video, photos, and audio resources	Directs students to information in multimedia format that they may never find on their own.
Syllabus of class	Provides easy access to outline of class activities and a timeline of class events.
Schedules	Keep the project on track and can be easily edited by the teacher if unforeseen events change the timeline.
Resource depot of tools	Puts all tools needed in an easy-to-find format that can be accessed when needed.
Group assignments	List responsibilities of group members in completing a group task so students can recall individual responsibilities.
Repository of podcasts	Class podcasts or teacher-made podcasts can be stored for easy accessibility by students.
Explanation of content	Contains synopsis of learned material covered in class with links to information for further study.
Instructions for assignments	Give students a place to find step-by-step directions for a project or assignment to keep them on task.
Parent information page	Easily edited Web page to keep parents updated on classroom activities.
Teacher tools	Provide a warehouse of teacher tools (graphic organizers, mapping tools, graphing tools, etc.) for easy accessibility or where teachers can access directions for use of technology equipment or software.

Figure 5.1. Uses for Library Wikis

LIBRARY WIKI RESOURCE	VALUE TO EDUCATOR
Repository of class notes and handouts	Stores documents (especially important for students who are absent or for students who have difficulty taking notes during lectures).
Storehouse for publishing finished student projects	Provides a place where student documents, videos, podcasts, or other assignments can be posted.
Classroom rules and procedures	Provide a place where students and parents can go to recall class expectations.
Professional development	Provides a warehouse of research, documents, articles, videos, etc., which teachers will find useful in solving classroom problems.
Lists of materials	Advertise and communicate new acquisitions, book reviews, and most popular novels (especially useful for media specialists).
Checklists and to-do lists	Assure students that they are not forgetting any important part of an assignment.

Figure 5.1. (*Continued*)

When creating a library wiki, one central rule applies that does not apply to any other type of wiki. Library wikis are only updated and edited by the wiki administrator. To protect and secure the material on the wiki, no editing privileges are given to users. This means the administrator becomes, in effect, a Web master, and all updating of the site is his or her responsibility. This is necessary because of the static nature of the content on this type of wiki. Putting this content in a wiki instead of a Web page gives the administrator the ease of editing the site quickly and regularly, where traditional Web pages cannot be changed as rapidly.

This does not mean, however, that collaboration is not part of the library wiki process. But the collaboration does not occur online as it does in other types of wikis. As a media specialist, it is imperative that I collaborate with classroom teachers before I create the library wiki to serve their students' needs. Classroom teachers will collaborate with other grade-level or department teachers to develop a wiki with the best resources available. The collaboration takes place behind the scenes of the library wiki; the collaboration in other wiki types occurs on the pages of the wiki itself. However, visible or not, collaboration is a big part of the process.

Collecting Resources for Library Wikis

Because the classroom teacher or media specialist is creating a wiki that will be a resource for its users, the vision and purpose of the wiki must be very clear to the creator from the beginning. You must know who will be using the wiki and for what purpose they will need the information it contains. The administrator of this type of wiki becomes the expert, and the content becomes the means to a specific end. Because of this, one must resist the temptation of using too many widgets, gadgets, and other superficial adornments that are not related to content, because they will confuse the users and impede the use of the wiki.

The creator of a library wiki who has a clear vision of the purpose for the wiki can find the best resources for assignments, tools that will be needed, and articles that need to be included. Using the vast array of resources available to teachers and media specialists in today's technological world, finding relevant and useful resources should not be difficult. However, here are some handy resources:

How to Find Primary Sources
<http://library.duke.edu/research/finding/primarysource.html> Search newspapers, government archives, and university libraries for primary sources.

100 Terrific Sites to Find Primary Source History Documents
<http://www.bachelorsdegreeonline.com/blog/2009/100-terrific-sites-to-find-primary-source-history-documents/> Features primary source documents, recordings, images and more.

Primary Sources in the Sciences
<http://guides.lib.msu.edu/page.phtml?page_id=2469> Primary sources in the sciences are different from primary sources in the humanities and social sciences, and this site tells you where to find them.

Physical Science, Math, and Technology Research: Supporting Data, Documents, and Artifacts <http://liblearn.osu.edu/guides/scitech/pg4.html>

Kathy Schrock's Navigating Primary Materials on the Internet <http://kathyschrock.net/navigating/> Organized by subject-specific sections.

Goodwin Library General Reference Center
<http://sites.google.com/site/goodwincollegereferencewiki/Home/reference-links> Almanacs, atlases, dictionaries, e-books, encyclopedias, and quotation sources.

Organization of the Library Wiki

Library wikis are about content and links to content. The best way to organize this type of wiki is to create a table of contents on the front page of the wiki that draws the user's attention immediately to the link that will deliver the content needed. A table of contents is made up of intrapage jumps that allow a reader to click on a link and jump to a section of text within the same page. It allows readers to quickly browse what is in the page and then jump to exactly what they want to read within the page. Some wikis will automatically build a table of contents for you from headers in the text. If not, you will have to simulate the same effect using HTML links to the section of page or subsequent pages. Here are some examples of great uses for library wikis in the school setting:

WIKI TITLE	URL	DESCRIPTION
Seventh Grade Research Project Wiki	<http://7thgraderesearch.pbworks.com/>	This wiki has step-by-step student directions and resources for a typical seventh-grade research paper assignment.
Industrial Revolution Wiki	<http://kmsamistad309.wikispaces.com/>	This wiki gives in-depth background information on the Industrial Revolution, with links to Web pages, video, and images that can be used for further study.
Bear Den Wiki	<http://bear-den.wikispaces.com/>	This classroom wiki gives students an overview of each unit studied, notes from class meetings, test preparation information, and rubrics on which they will be graded.
Mr. Bergmann's Science 8 Wiki	<http://bergmannscience.wikispaces.com/Science+8>	A classroom wiki that has a day-by-day schedule of classroom events and links to class notes and assignments.
Parenting Playfully Wiki	<http://www.classroom20wiki.com/>	This is one of the best uses for library wikis ever. This parent communication tool is beautifully crafted.
Web 2.0—Cool Tools for School Wiki	<http://cooltoolsforschools.wikispaces.com/>	This wiki is a storehouse of teacher tools for the classroom arranged in 18 categories.

Figure 5.2. Real-World Examples of Library Wikis

WIKI TITLE	URL	DESCRIPTION
Teaching and Learning with Digital Media Wiki	<http://teachandlearn.sydneyinstitute.wikispaces.net/>	A professional development site where teachers can learn about integration of digital media into their curriculum.
Dr. Reich's Chemistry Wiki	<http://reich-chemistry.wikispaces.com/>	Simple, no-frills wiki that gives chemistry students information on class schedules and assignments.
Online Tools Wiki	<http://educationalsoftware.wikispaces.com/Online+tools>	Great example of online tools teachers can easily access using a table to organize the content.
Exploring Geography Wiki	<http://exploringgeography.wikispaces.com/>	Nominated for an award in 2008, this geography site gives resources to students to complete an out-of-class project.
Special Education Needs Wiki	<http://usefulwiki.com/page/Special_Educational_Needs>	A wiki that provides the latest research for teachers of special needs students.
Teacher Portal Wiki	<http://teacherportal.wikispaces.com/>	This teacher resource portal demonstrates great organization by subject and grade level.
Tech2Learn Wiki	<http://tech2learn.wikispaces.com/>	Wrapped up in a dynamite front page, this wiki provides Web 2.0 resources and tools for easy use.
Young Adult Reading Lists Wiki	<http://yabooklists.wikispaces.com/>	On this wiki, a media specialist has listed popular, award-winning, or favorite young adult titles organized by genre.
CDS Professional Development Wiki	<http://cdspd.wikispaces.com/>	Arranged by topic, this wiki explores how technology can be integrated into the classroom.
Edorigami Wiki	<http://edorigami.wikispaces.com/wiki+mania>	Comprehensive listing of popular wiki sites such as Wikiquote, Wiktionary, Wikibooks, Wikicommons, Wikispecies, and Wikiversity.

Figure 5.2. (*Continued*)

The library wiki is a valuable tool for storing, organizing, classifying, and sharing resources with users. The amount of information that is available online is increasing exponentially. Keeping up in this new technological environment can be overwhelming and confusing for students and teachers alike. Wikis can impose structure to the available resources to help us make some order of the chaos of the Internet. Once the relevant information is organized, then we can use higher-level thinking skills to analyze, evaluate, and synthesize the information, which is education's ultimate goal.

CHAPTER 6

The Reciprocal Wiki

A reciprocal wiki is all about collaboration. Reciprocal wikis promote the synergetic effects that occur when students work as a team on a project. Whereas a library wiki essentially warehouses information, a reciprocal wiki invites user participation in completing a task, making lists, collecting documentation, and exchanging ideas. Whether educators create a wiki to team up with colleagues or interact with students, this tool holds great potential for the practice of virtual cooperative learning. Teachers will find that the use of wikis will support the integration of technology into their curriculum and facilitate instruction.

At schools today, e-mail is the primary method of communication a teacher utilizes to exchange information with colleagues. Teachers usually attach files they need to share to the e-mail. Some have ventured into the realms of Google Chat networking, but that typically is not teachers' first choice for communicating with colleagues. Reciprocal wikis, once they are introduced to teachers, find wide acceptance as a communication and file storage tool. The wiki has several major benefits that e-mail and file sharing do not have, and these special assets are what make it a powerful tool for education.

Although e-mail can be used for collaboration, because of its nature, e-mail becomes overwhelming when it is used for collaborative activity in a school setting. For example, team members forward and reply to notes, and each time everyone must go back and reread previous e-mails and responses to those e-mails to understand current e-mails. If someone forgets to click "Reply to all," the team may lose input from or alienate some of the team members. It quickly turns into a confused fiasco that hinders collaboration and results in a breakdown of the communication process. The net outcome is frustration for all and usually no one who is sure of the exact end product.

A wiki can simplify the collaboration process, and it does so without the gap in productivity associated with waiting for colleagues to read, reply, read other responses, reply again, and so on. A wiki is a static entity that can be accessed by many individuals who can edit, revise, and make additions to lists, calendars, plans, and projects. Tasks and revisions can be done simultaneously. Collaboration takes less time and is less complicated, and the end product is online for everyone to use and appreciate.

Wikis enable collaboration to take place at the same online location and automatically record revision history so you can review any editing that has taken place. This makes reverting to an earlier revision possible—even simple. Because of this function, the integrity of the original document is protected even after many changes and revisions. It is a perfect vehicle for educators who have no time to meet face-to-face but need to collaborate on joint resources and initiatives. When students are working on a group assignment and cannot meet outside of school to share ideas, a wiki is the best option for collaborating. If collaboration is the process of bringing people, ideas, best practices, and creation together, then wikis are the vehicles that make that process possible in today's educational setting.

Reciprocal wikis have many great educational uses, as the chart below demonstrates:

RECIPROCAL WIKI RESOURCE	VALUE TO EDUCATOR
Workshop for group projects	Provides structure to assure that all group members have the means to participate in the project.
Setting schedules and agendas	For meetings or timelines that need group input, a wiki can streamline the process.
Collaborative writing	Because one of today's important professional skills is learning to write reports as a team, wikis provide the setting to practice this skill.
Collaboration between teachers, departments, and schools	Provides opportunity for many minds to work together in addressing common goals and problems.
Resource lists	Wikis can store a collaborative and ever-growing list of common resources on various topics.

Figure 6.1. Uses for Reciprocal Wikis

A basic principle of education is that student learning is enhanced when students are actively engaged in the learning process. Learning is not a passive activity. Greater student engagement using wikis can result in greater learning outcomes. While students will have varied responses to using wikis—both positive and negative—most of my students report that the technology is easy to use and helped their learning. Although no published empirical evidence has been gathered on wiki effectiveness at this time, there are certainly observable benefits for student use of wikis. The lack of explicit documented evidence is not an indication that it does not work—rather that more studies need to be done. In my experience, students participate with this technology eagerly, and their performance is enhanced by its use. Wikis will not guarantee perfection, but they do promise participation in the learning process.

Organization of the Reciprocal Wiki

There are two basic types of structures for a reciprocal wiki. Both types have specific uses and outcomes. The first type allows anyone to view, download, and print from the wiki content, but only members may participate in editing and discussion boards. This gives the site control of who participates in the collaboration process and protects the integrity of the content while still allowing the wiki to be viewed and the content to be used by everyone. This type is good for class assignments, group projects, and teacher-to-teacher collaboration wikis.

The second type of reciprocal wiki allows anyone to edit content as well as view, download, and print the content. Any user may become a writer to the wiki and collaborator of content material. If this type of wiki is used, specific rules of collaboration need to be posted online at the wiki site to ensure consistency of content format. An example of such rules would look like this:

To share content, click on the page you want to edit. Once you are directed to that page, click on **Edit Page**. You may then:

- **Add a comment** by writing directly on the page. Please include your username in parentheses.* Do not forget to click **Save**!

- **Add a link** to a Web site by writing the name of the site, highlighting it, and clicking on the **Hyperlink** button in the **Edit** bar. You will then need to type in the address to the site. Please include your username in parentheses.* Click **Save**, and you are done!

- **Upload a lesson plan, form, or student writing sample** by clicking on the **Image and Files** tab on the sidebar under the **Insert Links** menu. Please do not copy and paste whole lesson plans onto the page; it is much easier to share and keep this wiki organized if you upload a separate document. Include a brief summary of the lesson with your document. Please include your username in parentheses.*

*When you include your username in parentheses, other members can contact you if they have questions or comments about your content. Thanks!

Here are some of the best examples of reciprocal wikis:

NAME OF WIKI	URL	DESCRIPTION
Litsource	<https://litsource.wikispaces.com/>	A reciprocal wiki where K–12 teachers can share lesson plans they recommend to teach reading.
Eight (or so) Easy 2.0 Pieces to Piece Together	<http://newtools workshop.wikispaces.com/>	Lists of links to educational Web 2.0 tools with opportunity to add to the list.
Bookleads	<http://bookleads.wikispaces.com/>	A collection of book blogs, reviews, author information, and reading resources for student use, with many areas to contribute your own resources.
Eat Me	<http://eatme.wikispaces.com/Apples>	A wiki that elicits written responses from students to convince other people to eat or not to eat certain foods.
Sample e-Portfolio Project	<http://pickeringportfolio.wetpaint.com/>	Wiki where student contributes multiyear contributions to a file of information.
eToolbox	<http://etoolbox.wikispaces.com/>	Resources list that advertises that new resources are added daily.
Holes	<http://stanleyyelnats.wikispaces.com/+Links>	Based on the popular novel, this wiki provides interactive student participation with the content of the book.
I Am Literate	<https://iamliterate.wikispaces.com/>	This wiki provides a growing list of 21st-century best practices in education.

Figure 6.2. Real-World Examples of Reciprocal Wikis

NAME OF WIKI	URL	DESCRIPTION
Collaboration Nation	<http://collaborationnation.wikispaces.com/>	This wiki showcases student digital stories and podcasts.
Classroom Google Earth	<http://classroomgoogleearth.wikispaces.com/?safe=on&safe=on&safe=on&safe=on&safe=on>	A wiki designed for both students and adults to share ideas about using Google Earth.
The Ultimate Teenage Reading List	<http://bhms-summer-read.wikispaces.com/>	A wiki created to give middle school students a place to read book reviews, discuss books they have read, and write poems.

Figure 6.2. (*Continued*)

The prevalent learning style today involves collaborative investigation, problem solving, and brainstorming. Business has embraced this team approach, because it is efficient and effective to accomplishing its goals. Education has embraced this approach, because our job is to prepare students to excel at the skills they need to succeed. Wikis are a potent tool to enhance the process of learning and one that will serve students well in the real world. It is a win-win combination.

CHAPTER 7

The Student-Produced Wiki

The student-produced wiki is another important type of wiki. It takes on the characteristics of an easy Web site. This function appeals to students because of their familiarity with the Internet. It gives them a hands-on opportunity to publish, collaborate on, and share information they deem as valuable. Because it takes them to a new level to exposure, they view the creation of a wiki as a real-world, noteworthy, and grown-up endeavor. Because they view the wiki creation as important, the assignment can become significant to them in the sense that they are likely to pay special attention to the mechanics of grammar and spelling, and it gives them a natural outlet for creativity and the higher-level thinking skills of analysis and synthesis of content material. Because of the collaborative nature of wikis, sharing their thoughts with others provides students with feedback that they see as more relevant than a grade on a classroom assignment. Teachers can use this intrinsic motivation to direct the student use of the wiki to express their opinions or warehouse information that they want to share, in a safe environment that teachers can monitor easily using supervisory controls that are available on most wiki user sites.

Wikis are much easier and quicker to create than traditional Web pages, and students are not hampered with writing code or creating templates to develop their online sites. Wikis do have some disadvantages, of course. Wikis are not as fancy and do not allow all of the special functions found on traditional Web pages. However, many elements can enhance student wikis so they appear dynamic and exciting and allow students to feel pride in their creation.

Setting Up Student Guidelines

Students need clear and precise directions and guidelines for wiki activities. As a school-supported assignment, wikis must promote learning, and the content of the wiki must conform to school norms. In sharing on collaborative wikis, a sense of constructive criticism must be cultivated and monitored. Here is a list of teacher activities that will promote student success with wikis:

TEACHING ACTIVITY	BENEFITS AND RESOURCES FOR ACTIVITY
Teach how wikis are structured by demonstration of example wikis. Show students how to access online tutorials about wikis that are found at most wiki host sites.	User host site online guides: PBWorks: <http://usermanual.pbworks.com/Workspace-Basics> WetPaint: <http://www.wetpaint.com/page/about> Wikispaces: <http://www.wikispaces.com/help+index>
Allow students to work in teams on a wiki project.	Students will experience the benefits of group authoring and editing.
Encourage students to use elements of wikis such as plug-in and widgets.	Students will want to make their wiki as useful and inviting as possible.
When working on group wiki, students need to reflect face-to-face as to the progress and future plans for the wiki on a weekly basis.	Students will want to communicate in traditional ways until they become comfortable with the online contact
Emphasize that this will be a document that might be read by many others, and so special attention needs to be given to mechanics.	Student will want to present their content using their best work.
Encourage students to make use of tags to make management of the wiki content easier.	Tags will track specific editing for additional ideas and content.
Assure students that frustration in technology projects is expected, and help from teachers and classmates is available for the asking.	This will prevent students from hitting a brick wall and stop progress on their wiki.

Figure 7.1. Activities To Promote Student Success Using Wikis

TEACHING ACTIVITY	BENEFITS AND RESOURCES FOR ACTIVITY
Set down a list of policies regarding unacceptable practices that will police wiki sites.	Students need to know that a wiki has rules that must be followed and it is not a re-placement for social networking sites.
Teachers must set themselves as admin-istrators of student wikis and monitor activities closely.	If students misuse the space, teachers have the ability to shut down the wiki completely.

Figure 7.1. (*Continued*)

Setting Up a Student-Produced Wiki

For best results, a teacher should set up student wikis (both group and individual), rather than allowing students to do so. With the teacher as administrator, there is more control over the methods and content of the wiki. Individual students, whether working independently or as a group, can then be listed as editors of the site. This gives the teacher the ability to monitor, edit, or delete undesirable content. Even students who do not have their own individual e-mail addresses can participate in this project. Directions for setting up a student-produced wiki using PBworks are listed below:

- Create a new wiki for a classroom by clicking on **Create a New Workplace**.

- On the **Sign Up** page, click on **Create an Academic Workspace**.

- Click on the **Free Basic Service** button.

- Type the name of the student wiki in the box provided. You may need to consult with the student(s) on an appropriate name.

- Click on button next to **For Education**.

- Under **Company Type**, list the level you are teaching.

- Under **Workspace Purpose**, list either **Easy Website** or **Collab-orative Workspace**, depending on the purpose of the site you are creating for your student(s).

- Click **NEXT** at the bottom right-hand side of page.

- Set the options **Who Can View This Workspace?** and **Who Can Edit This Workspace?** to the option **Only People I Invite or Ap-prove**. This will secure the site from vandalism, and approval for other users can be changed later.

- Click the box to agree to the PBworks terms of service.

- Click the bar on the bottom of the page that reads **Take Me to My Workspace**.

- On the sidebar of the new front page, click on **Settings** in the column at the top right-hand side.

- Under **Access Controls**, click on **Users**.

- Under **Add a User**, click on **Create Accounts for Your Students**.

- Enter the number of student accounts needed for this wiki, and set the permission level to **Editor**.

- Pick a user name for each user. The site will issue each user a unique password. This account list can be edited later.

- Click on **Create Accounts**.

- Print the list of account user names and passwords to keep for your records.

- Issue the URL, user names, and passwords to the students tied to the wiki site, and they are ready to begin.

Students should look at several student-produced wikis to use as models for their own creation. Here are some good examples:

NAME OF WIKI	URL	DESCRIPTION
My Side of the Mountain Wiki	<http://mysideofthemountain.wikispaces.com/>	Wiki contains student-made games, quizzes, puzzles, and summaries based on the Newbery Honor book.
Asalaamualiakum	<http://asalaamualiakum.wikispaces.com/>	A collection of student research on Pakistan.
Medical Maniacs	<http://codeblue.wikispaces.com/Medical+Maniacs>	As part of a sixth-grade pre-med class, students role play and explore different kinds of doctor specialties.
Wee Web Wonders	<http://weewebwonders.synthasite.com/>	An interactive site to showcase creative uses by students of some of the major web tools.
Properties of Water	<http://desbuffalo.wikispaces.com/%2AProperties+of+Water>	Fifth-graders gather facts and write creatively about water.

Figure 7.2. Real-World Examples of Student-Produced Wikis

NAME OF WIKI	URL	DESCRIPTION
Digital Literacy	<http://milliswiki.wikispaces.com/>	High school students combine efforts to describe uses of Web 2.0 tools.
Let's Go West	<http://gowest.wikispaces.com/>	A third-grade study of westward expansion along the Oregon Trail.
Teenager's Guide to Everywhere	<http://teenagersguideto everywhere.wikispaces.com/ >	Resource file for middle school research project on interesting places.
History Fair Project	<http://victoriaaurorahistory fairproject.wetpaint.com/>	A report about women in the American Revolution and Civil War.
Help Save Darfur	<http://savedarfurnhs.wetpaint.com/>	Ways to help the current Darfur crisis and what one school did to contribute to a solution.
Our Environment	<http://ourenvironment.tk/>	This wiki points out how the planet is dealing with pollution in its ecosystem. This wiki has been translated into more than 30 languages.
Booktalking with You	<http://booktalk.pbworks.com/>	Students post book reviews and podcasts for teens and young adults.

Figure 7.2. (*Continued*)

Building a Learning Community

Students will not have an immediate understanding of how and why wikis build a learning community. It is important that teachers take time to instill the value of wikis and how they support learning. Students will be familiar with other Web 2.0 tools such as Facebook, Twitter, and blogs. A distinction needs to be made that wikis have a different purpose when used in the classroom. Students need to be made aware that the functions of editing, revising, and collaborating make the wiki a powerful learning tool. Students need an explanation of how collaboration of thoughts, ideas, and reflections builds synergy that creates deeper understanding of the content. Only with this knowledge of the power of the wiki will students realize how wikis go beyond other social networking sites and engage people in higher-level thinking that includes analyzing, evaluating, and synthesizing information. Once students clearly see this wiki influence on how they learn, they can use wikis to their best advantage as a collaboration tool for many years to come.

CHAPTER 8

Implementing
Activities

When wikis are integrated into a curriculum, they can be a great motivator for student learning. They allow students to be creative and innovative and encourage their interaction with other students, as well as with the content being studied. They promote communication between students, teachers, and parents. They utilize Web 2.0 technology to make learning more interesting and tap into today's learners' natural gravitation to technology as a fun activity.

Wikis make it easy for teachers to monitor student progress in a way that is nonthreatening to students. They provide a way to manage and store classroom documents that can be retrieved upon demand. They provide a forum to post class assignments. They facilitate group projects and add the dimension of classroom discussion and debate to the assignment that does not usually take place beyond the walls of the classroom.

There are some special activities that classroom teachers can employ to assure that wikis become embedded into the classroom experience and are not relegated to just an add-on assignment.

- Take time to introduce the wiki. Students need to be comfortable with wikis to utilize them successfully. You will need to spend one class period to walk them through its features and potential uses. A short video to use as an introduction can be found at: <http://www.commoncraft.com/video-wikis-plain-english>

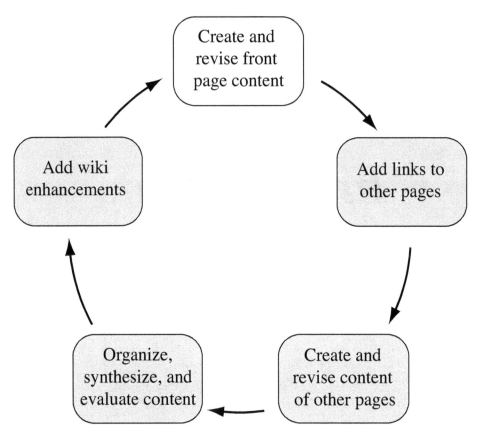

Figure 8.1. Cycle of Wiki Creation and Revision

- To use a wiki most effectively, students need to be in command of the content. Teachers can monitor wikis for inappropriate entries and misuse of the space, but the content needs to be the students' domain.

- Make the assignment open-ended. Wikis are always a work in progress.

- Do not impose strict rules and patterns of usage. Familiarize students with the endless cycle of wiki creation and revision that is necessary to keep the wiki current.

- Wiki user sites offer e-mail notification features for the administrator. Use e-mail notification of changes to monitor student sites.

- Less is more; motivation decreases when there are too many assignments or too many discussion questions.

TYPE OF INVOLVEMENT	METHOD OF INVOLVEMENT
Individual pages	Ask each student to create a wiki page, posting information about their interests and what they hope to learn from the class. Be sure to comment on the pages, and engage students by referencing their personal interests in discussions. Use this as an easy icebreaker to have students get to know each other.
Self-selection	List weekly discussion topics on your wiki, have students select a topic and lead the discussion.
Group brainstorming	Have students brainstorm possible discussion topics on the wiki and lead one discussion per week.
Easy poll and survey	Embed an online poll to create an easy online poll in your wiki. Use the poll to make class decisions or share opinions anonymously.
Community problem solving	Ask students to answer a homework question on the wiki, providing only part of the solution. Have each student respond and grade the final answer.
Asynchronous open-ended discussions	Ask students to prepare a list of questions for a guest speaker. Use the gabbly chat plug-in to talk with everyone on the wiki page, or embed a meebo chat to communicate one-on-one with students.
Class notes	Each week assign one student to write up the class notes, including important points and class discussion. Be sure to comment on the notes, and add additional insight from the lesson.
Wiki pairs	Ask students to partner with another student in class. These partners should comment on each other's work, brainstorm new ideas, and generally help each other. Private wiki pages make it easy to create pages that only two students can edit.
Wiki group work	Create a page that only members of a group can access, and monitor their progress on a research task over time. You can give feedback immediately and see who is pulling their weight.
Publicize good work	Post student work online as an example or archive to show course expectations. You can easily create public wiki pages in a private PBwiki (this is a free feature of 2.0 wikis).
Individual observations	Students record specific examples of their internship and reflect how these experiences relate to current course material. This can be private or include wiki-pair or teacher feedback.
Web research	Students work on a research project, summarizing their findings on a wiki page and listing their Web sources, articles, and so on on the wiki. Peers can comment on or add to the page.

Figure 8.2. Twelve Ways To Get Students Involved in Your Wiki

- As your usage of wikis grows, use wikis across age groups, classes, courses, or distance.

- Allow students to comment on wikis of other groups or individuals.

- Be as clear as possible about what counts as acceptable collaboration. Outline ways of acknowledging dissatisfaction.

- In assessments of wiki assignments, encourage creativity and innovative thinking. Be clear about the assessment criteria and that they may shift, because some classes evolve more quickly than others do.

- Make clear to students the purpose for using the wiki in the curriculum of your classroom.

- Align student wiki assignments with learning objectives.

- Build in milestones on editing skills where possible.

- Reward both the product (pages produced) and the process (edits, messages, and other features) of developing a wiki.

- Be prepared to be overwhelmed by the creativity and imagination of some students.

Parent Involvement

Parents will probably not be familiar with wikis and may have questions about their use with students. Communication of what you want to accomplish with a student wiki and how your plan will accomplish those goals will help them understand this technology. A sample letter to help introduce parents to the use of wikis follows:

STUDENT PARTICIPATION IN COLLABORATIVE WIKI PROJECTS

Parents:

During this school year, your child will have an opportunity to participant in an online collaborative project involving the use of wikis. A wiki is an Internet site that allows communication and collaboration between the teacher and individual students or groups of students. Using a wiki, students can communicate and share ideas, research, or projects with others. Using wikis with group project activities, group members are able to access, edit, revise, and enhance each other's work. It is a work model that the business world has employed for the last decade, and it will provide students with practice in real-world technology use that will prepare them for future employment in today's high-tech world.

You have probably become distrustful of some Internet social networking sites that have shown themselves to be a dangerous place for children. Let me assure you that your student's participation in this endeavor will be constantly monitored, and access to their contributions will be secure and can only be accessed by the teacher, the parent, and other students who are collaborating on the project. An important goal of using wikis in our classroom is to help students learn through experiences how to use the Internet in a safe environment to share information and collaborate with others. This letter is being sent to you so that you know what we are planning to do, assure you that your child's safety online is foremost in our plans, and to obtain your permission for your child to participate.

We will be using online wiki sites to let students SAFELY share their work and ideas with other students as well as with their teacher. We will share these projects privately with other classes over the Internet and with parents, but we will not share the projects publicly on the Internet. To protect student privacy and ensure safety throughout these projects, we will:

1. Only use student first names, or online nicknames, in identifying student work and ideas.
2. Not use pictures of individual students.
3. Closely monitor wikis produced by students on an ongoing basis.

If you have questions about our projects, please let me know. I will be in contact with you with information regarding your student's wiki so that you will also have the capability to monitor their progress. Please complete, sign, and return the bottom of this form to me as soon as possible.
Thank you.

_____

_____ YES, my child has my permission to participate in teacher-moderated, Internet-based collaborative projects using wikis.
_____ NO, my child does not have permission to participate in these activities.

Date: _____

Student Name: Student Signature:

_____   _____

Parent Name: Parent Signature:

_____   _____

Teacher-To-Teacher

Teachers collaborate using wikis to share ideas, strategies, and resources. Here are some resources that contain teacher experiences with using wikis:

- *Wikis in Education* <http://wikisineducation.wetpaint.com/page/How+we+use+wikis+in+class?t=anon> Wiki where teachers collaborate on the use of wikis in the classroom
- *The Wiki Way: Creating and Facilitating an Online Learning Environment Using Wikis* <http://rachelboyd.wikispaces.com/wiki+workshop> Ideas for possible uses of wikis in the classroom
- *A Collaboration of Sites and Sounds* <http://www.readwritethink.org/lessons/lesson_view.asp?id=979> A model lesson plan for using wikis in the classroom
- *Collaborating, Writing, Linking: Using Wikis to Tell Stories Online* <http://www.readwritethink.org/lessons/lesson_view.asp?id=1087> Lesson plan for implementing online reading and writing

Administrative Wikis

Administrative use of the wiki is to warehouse schedules, documents, directives, lists, and calendars in one place for easy reference by teachers and staff. Instead of e-mails or documents on individual teacher computers that may or may not be the latest version of one of these important notices, administrators can keep an updated wiki, giving only authorized personnel access to its content. The administrator can then be assured that the staff has immediate access to current and accurate information they need in their classrooms. In implementing this wiki, administration is also building the use of technology into their skill set, and teachers will become more familiar with wiki use and will become comfortable enough to use it in their classrooms.

Assessing Wikis

Assessing wiki usage is a tricky business. Because the teacher has made it an integral part of the curriculum, it needs to be assessed for completion, accuracy, and content without infringing on the elements of collaboration, creativity, and innovation. Therefore, the assessment scheme must be a general matrix that can be adapted to whatever student wikis become in their transformation over a period of time. A model of such a rubric is:

WIKI ASSESSMENT RUBRIC

_____ 15 points **COLLABORATION** The wiki is a collaborative endeavor. Several participants have contributed, and each group member has contributed to the project.

_____ 10 points **ORGANIZATION** A table of contents is used, and headings and underlining are used appropriately.

_____ 15 points **VISUAL APPEARANCE** Graphics are used as needed but are not used excessively nor distract from the wiki content.

_____ 10 points **LINKS TO OTHER SOURCES** An effective wiki hyperlinks sources and gives readers additional information about the content. Because most people tend to not trust wikis (authors are unknown to them), you can include hyperlinks to supporting material to make your wiki more authoritative and effective.

_____ 15 points **ORIGINAL WORK** The well-written wiki summarizes and organizes information. Sources must be cited and cannot be copied from other sources word-for-word.

_____ 10 points **MECHANICS (GRAMMAR AND SPELLING)** The audience of your wiki is potentially anyone and everyone. People are judged by their proper use of language.

_____ 25 points **CONTENT** The content of the wiki must relate to the assignment topic

_____ **TOTAL POINTS**

OPTIONAL EXTRA CREDIT

_____ up to 20 points **USE OF AUDIOVISUAL** The wiki uses sound, animated graphics, video, and other elements to increase the user's engagement with the wiki site, thereby increasing the potential learning.

_____ up to 20 points **USE OF ADDITIONAL WEB 2.0 TOOLS** Other Web2.0 technologies can be integrated into your wiki page. Such additions will be considered innovative and enhancing to your wiki. These technologies include RSS feeds, videos, podcasts, widgets, gadgets, and a variety of other tools you may find.

Other wiki assessment models can be found online at the following sites:

URL	DESCRIPTION
<http://www.readwritethink.org/lesson_images/lesson979/wikirubric.pdf>	Simple matrix format with a five-point grading criteria
<http://edorigami.wikispaces.com/file/view/wiki+editting+rubric+v2.pdf>	Rubric for editing rubrics is linked to Bloom's taxonomy
<http://wikisineducation.wetpaint.com/page/Grading+Rubric+Template>	Very simple rubric for wikis using a four-point grading criteria
<http://cache-www.intel.com/cd/00/00/36/20/362077_362077.doc>	Content-specific wiki grading rubric that can be adapted to your content area

Figure 8.3. Wiki Assessment Rubrics

As a media specialist, I have made great efforts to be a useful resource on Web 2.0 tools. More than any other new technology, teachers have asked for my assistance in establishing classroom and student-produced wikis and creating a library wiki of resources to support a specific assignment they have planned. I have seen firsthand students' excitement at creating their own wikis and in their interaction with peers and others in collaboration and conversation about the topic they are studying. It is indeed a powerful addition to a teacher's bag of tricks in the classroom.

CHAPTER 9

Special Uses for Wikis

Wikis can be impressive in their implementation with students who have learning problems, are academically talented, or are learning English as a second language. Many educators have found success in introducing the wiki tool into their special curricula. With the prominent policy of inclusion in today's classrooms, even teachers who do not specialize in exceptional student education (ESE) find that the aids on a wiki that provide help for their students with learning problems can be a tremendous help to their regular students as well. Because these special education wikis are designed to help learners with special needs achieve a higher level of personal self-sufficiency and success in school, teachers find that the methods and strategies they contain can also be beneficial to all students. Exploring how these special uses for wikis have enhanced learning with these students can help us all understand the power of the wiki.

Wikis and the Exceptional Student

Students who have learning disabilities have special needs that must be accommodated in order for learning to take place. Such students exhibit difficulty in one or more of the following areas:

- Learning disabilities
- Developmental delays
- Emotional or behavioral problems
- Communication disorders
- Hearing impairments
- Visual impairments
- Physical disabilities

Many tools for these students can be warehoused on a library wiki to facilitate their learning.

- Organizational tools such as graphic organizers can be made available.
- Teacher-produced and student-produced podcasts of classroom notes and discussions can be posted.
- Students with severe learning disabilities can document class trips within the community in both words and pictures.
- Study tools such as flash cards, PowerPoints presentations, and on-line quizzes can facilitate student assignments.
- Links to e-books as well as text-to-speech and speech-to-text tools could be collected to help students with reading or vision problems.
- To aid in doing research, a wiki can provide links to search tools, note-taking tools, and sample papers.
- Math tutorials could be easily accessed in video, audio, or written format.
- Worksheets, games, and other activities related to class content could extend the student's learning beyond the classroom.
- Study guides and study strategies could help parents with the student's at-home learning.
- Teachers can create specially formatted writing templates so students can download and print at-home assignments.

Here is a list of exceptional wikis created for exceptional students and their teachers:

NAME OF WIKI	URL	DESCRIPTION
Technology Toolkit	<http://udltechtoolkit.wikispaces.com/>	A huge array of tools for the exceptional student, their teachers, and parents
Safeway Wiki	<http://safeway.pbworks.com/>	Students comment on their trip to a local grocery store
Learning Fun for Students	<http://matnonline.pbworks.com/Learning-Fun-for-Students>	Compilation of student-friendly interactive learning links
Mr. Barnes' Virtual Language Arts Class	<http://middleschoolworld.editme.com/>	Good example of how wikis can keep students organized and on task

Figure 9.1. Real-World Examples of Wikis for Exceptional Students

Many teachers of exceptional students are looking for new tools and strategies to meet state standards, motivate students, create an environment that encourages positive social interaction, and create self-motivation and active engagement in learning. The wiki is one of those tools because of its inherent use of interactive content, resource sharing, and convenience. Here are some resources ESE teachers could use in the creation of a classroom wiki:

Alphabet and Phonics Worksheets
<http://specialed.about.com/od/worksheets/a/alphabets.htm>

Resources for Teachers
<http://specialed.about.com/od/worksheets/a/alphabets.htm>

Graphic Organizers
<http://www.teachervision.fen.com/graphic-organizers/printable/6293.
    html?detoured=1>

Printable Writing Paper
<http://www.first-school.ws/theme/printables/writing-paper/hand
    writing.htm>

Wikis and the ESOL Student

English for speakers of other languages (ESOL) is called by several names, but all of these titles describe the task of teaching students whose native language is one other than English. ESOL students bring with them different cultural perceptions and communication styles that need to be addressed by the ESOL teacher. Many times ESOL teachers do not speak English as their native language themselves, which adds another layer to the difficult task of integrating the ESOL student. The use of the wiki in this teaching task appeals to ESOL students, because the information it contains is easily accessed, and the tools found on the wiki are just-in-time tools that students will need during their adventure of learning English. Some of the resources the ESOL teacher may include in the wiki are:

- Vocabulary lists sorted by category
- Pronunciation guides with audio files
- Podcasts
- Videos
- Spelling rules and grammar rules
- Worksheets, documents, and assignments
- Study strategies, printable flash cards, and online quizzes

- Text-to-speech and speech-to-text tools
- Information about the class for parents written in several languages as needed

Some great resources for an ESOL wiki are:

Links of Interest to Students and Teachers of English as a Second Language
<http://iteslj.org/links/>

Interesting Thongs for ESL Students
<http://www.manythings.org/>

20-Minute ESL Lessons
<http://www.esl-lab.com/vocab/index.htm>

Here are some successful ESOL wikis in use today:

NAME OF WIKI	URL	DESCRIPTION
1312 Class Wiki	<http://wiki.utep.edu/display/ESOL1312Fall2009/Welcome+to+your+ESOL+1312+class+wiki;jsessionid=2A894FC9E0338D05C215B10361B5175E>	This wiki is used as an online journal for ESOL students
Talk About Primary	<http://talkaboutprimarymfl.wiki-spaces.com/>	Sharing links to ESOL sites
English VG1	<http://englishvg1.wikispaces.com/>	Links to understanding U.S. culture
HispaLegere	<http://hispalegere.wikispaces.com/>	Written in Spanish, this wiki helps teach the English language

Figure 9.2. Real-World Examples of Wikis for ESOL Students

Teaching Foreign Languages Using Wikis

Educators who teach foreign languages use many the same approaches to teaching a new language that teachers use in teaching English to ESOL students. Foreign-language teachers must teach not only the basics of the language, but also the culture and communication style of the language studied. The same reasons that ESOL wikis work so well with those students also work for students of foreign languages. However, besides the basic wiki uses, students who are learning a new language also need easy access to:

- Vocabulary lists that give easy access to foreign language keywords and translations
- Pronunciation guides with audio files that help students with correct word pronunciation
- Podcasts and videos of the culture of the country where the language is in use
- Widgets such as currency converters and world time clocks to bring authenticity to the language being learned
- Worksheets, documents, and assignments posted by the teacher
- Study strategies, printable flash cards, and online quizzes, which keep the student organized and current
- Text-to-speech and speech-to-text tools
- Information about the class for parents

Here are some successful foreign-language wikis in use today:

NAME OF WIKI	URL	DESCRIPTION
Ah-Bon French	<http://ah-bon-french.wiki spaces.com/>	Middle school French class site
French Resources and Activities Wiki	<http://mariajose83.wikispaces. com/Quelques+liens+utiles>	Multimedia wiki about the French language
LHS French Classes	<http://lhsfrenchclasses.wiki spaces.com/>	Class assignments, documents, video, and audio files
Madame Space	<http://madamekrause.wiki spaces.com/>	Online workspace for French classes
Conversation Station	<http://teensntech.wikispaces. com/Conversation+Stations>	Demonstrates how podcasts can be used to teach languages
Spanish	<https://spanish-farb.wikispaces. com/>	Middle school Spanish wiki
Mr. Craft's Wiki	<http://chriscraft.wetpaint.com/>	Wiki that encourages student collaboration in learning Spanish or Latin
Spanish Classes	<http://www.maztravel.com/ wiki/Spanish%20Classes>	Comprehensive site for learning Spanish

Figure 9.3. Real-World Examples of Wikis for Foreign-Language Students

Wikis and the Gifted Student

Academically gifted students sometimes present challenges to their teachers, who want to keep them engaged and motivated in learning not only the mandated basic benchmarks but also enhancements of that knowledge that encourages creativity and higher-level thinking. Wikis are a natural vehicle to inspire and motivate these students. They tend to enjoy learning exploring, creating, and collaborating with wikis. Not only do wikis present an extended opportunity to work in partnership with their peers who share the same intellectual curiosity about things, but wikis also create social networking opportunities that provide a platform for synergy that comes when these gifted students combine forces. Teachers of these students learn quickly to introduce the basics of collaborative student-produced wikis and appropriate topics for those wikis, and then monitor their activities online and watch the creativity flow. All three types of wikis work well with gifted students, and the addition of multimedia to the wiki stimulates the creativity and higher-level thinking that are innate in this type of student. Wikis provide an opportunity for academically talented students to accelerate learning and enrich the subject areas they study.

NAME OF WIKI	URL	DESCRIPTION
Virtual Zoo	<http://talentedandgifted.wikispaces.com/Virtual+Zoo+-+Summer+08>	Primary students use multimedia to report
The Death Penalty	<http://web-projects.wikispaces.com/The+Death+Penalty+in+America>	High school gifted students' assignment
Library Zone	<http://libraryzone.wikispaces.com/Presentations>	A collection of multimedia reports by intermediate gifted students
Kmsamistad	<http://kmsamistad309.wikispaces.com/>	Student-generated content about the Amistad incident and the Industrial Revolution
Forensic Science	<http://weewebwonders.pbworks.com/Forensic-Science>	Student-created wiki utilizing multimedia and interactive games to report on the topic

Figure 9.4. Real-World Examples of Wikis for Gifted Students

CHAPTER 10

The Bottom Line

There is always a bottom line. In education, the bottom line always comes down to: "How much time will this take?" and "How much will this cost?" Wikis are free to educational users and, after the initial set-up, are fast and convenient to implement. Wikis are indeed powerful tools for learning. Are they extra work for the teacher? Yes, but the many benefits they provide make wikis an almost joyous undertaking. As a vehicle that stimulates student motivation, creativity, and higher-level thinking, teachers consider wikis a necessary means to an important end. This chapter explains a few points that will become essential as you enter the wiki world and as you begin to use wikis with your students.

Copyright Considerations

Copyright rules and regulations are often confusing. We all know that original written material is copyrighted material. Many people wonder whether everything found online is copyrighted. The short answer is yes; you should consider almost everything in print or online to be copyright protected. Even if the copyright symbol (©) is not present, you should assume that the material is copyrighted. Materials created since 1978 have protection from the moment the work takes tangible form—regardless of whether a copyright notice is evident and whether the individual has filed an application with the United States Copyright Office. For works created and published before 1978, copyright will be in place for 75 years from the time of publication or copyright renewal. By law, one cannot infringe on the rights of copyrighted materials—meaning you cannot use the material without specific author permission. However, certain exceptions to the steadfast copyright regulations are in place for materials that are used for educational purposes and not for profitable gain. The U.S.

government has established special permissions for educators to make use of copyrighted material for educational purposes. Fair use guidelines, or exceptions to the copyright usage regulations, give teachers and students limited permission to use some copyrighted materials in class projects. There are four standards that educators must adhere to in order to determine whether fair use guidelines apply to their situation:

- **What is the purpose of using the material?** Copying and using selected parts of copyrighted works for specific educational purposes qualifies as fair use, especially if the copies are used for temporary purposes.

- **What is the nature of the material you want to use?** For copying paragraphs from a copyrighted source, fair use applies and it is allowed. For copying an entire chapter, fair use may be questionable.

- **How much of the material do you intend to use?** When duplicating excerpts that are short in relation to the entire copyrighted work and do not reflect the "essence" of the work, it is regarded as fair use.

- **Will your use of the material have any effect on the marketability of the work?** Use of copyrighted material must not infringe on the marketability of the material. If there will be no reduction in sales because of copying or distribution, the fair use exemption is likely to apply. Teachers need to pay close attention to this standard, because it is the most important of the four tests for fair use.

An entire look at the fair use copyright exemptions for educators can be found at: <http://www.copyright.gov/circs/circ21.pdf>

To be absolutely safe in the use of copyrighted images, documents, articles, and so on in a wiki, make sure that information is cited and, if possible, ask the author for permission to cite. If you or your students make the educational purpose clear to the author, most likely he or she will allow usage. If permission is not granted, do not use that material. It is really quite simple: if you have doubts about the material's legitimate use, do not use it.

Teach students how to cite information correctly and insist that they do so. Even primary students can be taught to understand the concept of borrowing and sharing, and it is never too early to learn a life skill that will serve them well for many years. Cite sources yourself to model this important skill, and students will quickly catch on to its importance. Here are some great sites to make citations easy to do:

- The Importance of Citing Sources <http://www.teach-nology.com/tutorials/teaching/citing/print.htm>

- Son of Citation Machine <http://citationmachine.net/>

- Cite Those Sources <http://www.readwritethink.org/lessons/les son_view.asp?id=158>

- Censorship and Responsibility <http://hums3001.unsw.wikispaces. net/>

Protecting Students Online

Educators know that we must take certain steps to protect students online from threats. We are responsible to ensure that students interact on the Internet in a safe and secure environment and to closely monitor that environment. Wikis provide safeguards that assure teachers and parents that students can use collaborative Internet tools without exposure to online predators and unsuitable materials. Here are the unique qualities that wikis provide to make certain that students are safe:

- **Wikis are private**—Because you make student wikis private, it eliminates the possibility of student interaction with the public. This protected environment is only accessible to those parents, other students, and teachers who have permission to collaborate with students.

- **No personal information is online**—Teachers must insist that students use only their first names, or online user names, and never upload personal photos. Students should be encouraged to use avatars in place of photos.

- **Links that students use in their wiki contributions are monitored**—Students need to be encouraged to link only to internal wiki pages or files. For older students, linking is a great way to teach information literacy and determine which sites are credible and which are not; however, teachers need to keep a vigil on what Internet sites students link on their wikis.

- **Teachers can enable e-mail notifications to monitor student editing**—Wikis can send e-mail notification to teachers whenever a student revises or edits a wiki. As the administrator of the wiki, the teacher can access the history of who has revised any portion of the material on a wiki.

- **Security tools are built into the wiki**—PBworks, as well as other wiki providers, have many security controls to make the student wiki as open or closed as desired. Make sure you understand the tools before implementing them in your class. A guide to how the security features work and how they are accessed can be found at: <http:// usermanual.pbworks.com/Educational-Editions-Access-Controls>

- **Parents sign a permission form**—An example of a parent permission letter is found in chapter 8. Educating parents about why and how their student will use a collaborative wiki is imperative to its success.

- **Parents are invited to join**—Encourage parents to participate; have them subscribe to the wiki.

- **Teachers can give students a pat on the back**—Show off your students' successes while reminding parents what their children are working on.

- **Online mentors can be used**—Locate parents or teachers who are willing to read student pages and posts and comment on them. This expands the classroom discussion and lets the students know that their work is representative of real-world collaborative practices. Include the school principal!

A few final notes about safety; if you use a public computer:

- Do not save login information.
- Make sure to exit your e-mail application before you leave.
- Use Tools to erase your Internet browsing history. To do this:
  - Click on **Tools** on the menu bar
  - Click on **Delete Browsing History**
  - Click on the **Delete History** button

The Parent Connection

Most parents will not have the faintest idea of what a wiki is, so a brief explanation to them of what it is and how their student will be using it is essential. Giving parents information on the wiki's purpose is and how you plan to use it with your students will educate them on this 21st-century tool. Assure them that you will take precautions to keep the wiki site private and that the wiki is not accessible to the dangers lurking on the open Internet. Inform them that student content on the wiki will be continuously monitored and invite them to access the wiki themselves (you will need the parent's e-mail address to do this). Using this pre-lesson communication will avoid many anxious phone calls later on and might even pique parental interest in the content on the wiki. Wikis are new to most people, so a letter of introduction will be welcome. Look for an example of a parent introductory letter in chapter 8.

The Good News and the Bad News

At the end of this comprehensive look at the creation and use of wikis in the classroom, the good news is that you have discovered uses for perhaps the most powerful Web 2.0 tool for your students' learning experience. In our high-tech world today, students need to learn how to use the technology tools that will not only make learning more enjoyable for them but also give them real-world skills in what is already embraced as standard operating procedure. The bad news is that you will spend a lot of your time during the next few months finding new and exciting uses for wikis in your school and classroom. However, as fun and as useful as wikis can be, maybe the bad news is not so bad after all.

Works Cited

"Enabling Student Collaboration for Learning." *Teaching and Learning with Technology Center.* October 2003. Georgia State University, Web. 7 Dec 2009. http://www2.gsu.edu/~wwwltc/howto/enablestudentcollab. htm

Horn, Ilana. "Teacher Collaboration and Ambitious Teaching: Reflections on What Matters." *New Horizons for Learning.* April 2006. New Horizons in Education, Web. 7 Dec 2009. http://www.newhorizons.org/spneeds/ inclusion/staff/horn.htm

Inger, Morton. "Teacher Collaboration in Secondary Schools." *National Center for Research in Vocational Education.* December 1993. University of California Berkeley, Web. 7 Dec 2009. http://vocserve.berkeley.edu/cen terfocus/CF2.html

Kohm, Barbara, and Beverly Nance. "Creating Collaborative Cultures." *Educational Leadership* 67.2 (2009): 67–72. *Professional Development Collection.* EBSCO. Web. 8 Dec. 2009. http://search.ebscohost.com/ login.aspx?direct=true&db=tfh&AN=44511206&site=ehost-live

Leonard, Lawrence, and Pauline Leonard. "The Continuing Trouble with Collaboration: Teacher Talk." *Current Issues in Education.* 2003. Current Issues in Education, Web. 7 Dec 2009. http://cie.asu.edu/volume6/ number15/#school

McClure, Carla. "The Benefits of Teacher Collaboration." *District Administrator.* September 2008. Professional Media Group, Web. 7 Dec 2009. http://www.districtadministration.com/viewarticle.aspx?articleid=1682

Parker, Kevin, and Joseph Chao. "Wiki as a Teaching Tool." *Interdisciplinary Journal of Knowledge and Learning Objects.* 2007. Web. 7 Dec 2009. http://www.ijklo.org/Volume3/IJKLOv3p057-072Parker284.pdf

Index

About the Author

Kay Teehan is a 40-year veteran teacher and media specialist. She has earned National Board of Professional Teaching Standards certification, a BS in education, and an MA in educational technology. She is a Florida Master Digital Educator, Discovery Education STAR Educator, and formally was an advisor to Channel One network news. She has taught at every level, including college education courses. She is the author of *Digital Storytelling: In and Out of the Classroom* (2006) and *Peering into Technology* (2007). Presently she is a media specialist in Polk County, Florida.